I Call Him KING

by

Quiet Storm

Esquire Publications

"Your Voice In Print!"

Esquire Publications
P. O. Box 352234
Palm Coast, FL 32135

Esquire Publications
P. O. Box 352234
Palm Coast, FL 32135
www.esquirepublications.com
Tel: 1-800-501-7640

"I Call Him King"

Edited By: Christine G. Broome
Cover Art: Varunish
Designer: Brian F. Scrivener

Library of Congress Cataloging-in-Publication Data

Library of Congress Control Number: 2012945720

ISBN: 9781626204324

Printed in the United States of America

I Call Him KING

by

Quiet Storm

Never allow someone to be your priority
While allowing yourself to be their option

MARK TWAIN

Table of Contents

1

⚸

THE INTRO

Let us not give up meeting together, as some are in the habit of doing,
but let us encourage one another—and all the more as you see the Day
approaching.

HEBREWS 10:25

"Hey Mommy, let's go to McDuff's Sports Bar. Everybody goes there now," Arielle requested.

"Hmmm, I don't know. I'm okay with having dinner right here at La Cage. Besides, you know I don't like hanging out at places like that and I haven't been to a sports bar in a long time," I said.

"Oh come on, please! Your gonna like it and this place is dead," Arielle coaxingly said.

"Yeah, it kinda is and there isn't anything else to do. I guess so, but I don't want to stay long, maybe to have one drink and that's it."

"Mommy, it's Saturday night, stop acting like an old maid!"

"Whatever!" I responded.

Pulling into the parking lot of McDuff's, I was lucky to find a spot by the door as someone was backing out. The place was packed. There were two entrances and both had people standing in front of them as if they were waiting to get in. We had to keep saying "excuse me" to get through. I just wanted to find a seat so I could people watch and as soon as someone got up, I sat down at the bar while Arielle strolled her way through the crowd to meet her friends. She was MIA for at least 20 minutes and then came back with a caramel colored brother that stood about my height of 5'3". He had glassy eyes, long eyelashes and a bright smile.

"Mommy this is Damon, Robbie's and Randy's dad." I knew Robbie and Randy because they went to school with my girls.

" Damon, this is my mom, Storm."

With a deep voice, Damon extended his hand to me.

"Nice to meet you."

"You too, I've heard a lot about you," I responded.

"All good I hope?" he asked staggering.

"It was," I smiled.

To be honest, all I ever heard about Damon was that he was a nice man, could build houses, was funny, and was in love with my twin baby girl, BJ, and he would call her his daughter. A year back the girls had taken the twins over to his house so all the kids could go swimming in his pool.

I sat back on my stool and watched people dance, argue, kiss…just a little bit of everything was going on. The place was loud with many conversations filling the air along with music blasting through the speakers. I had not been to a sports bar in over three years. It was so crowded that you had to literally touch shoulders with people just to be able to get to the bathroom. It certainly was a popular spot and it seemed as though all of Lake Shores was in this place.

It was just about 2AM and McDuff's was about to close. Everyone started dispersing into the parking lot and the sidewalk to continue with their socializing. Arielle, Damon, his roommate, Aaron, and I crowded into a circle and talked briefly. I asked Damon how his sons were doing. He stated that they were doing well. I then looked over at Aaron, remembering him as someone I had seen being around my other daughter, Lisa. I let him know that I was her mother. We had that "oh wow, okay" brief moment laugh and then Damon intervened by stating how good he could fry fish at his house. Aaron cosigned.

"Yeah, everybody comes over there after hours to get his fish. It's like another party," said Aaron.

Apparently, this was one of the things that Damon was known for.

"So, what's your real name?" Damon asked in a slurred speech.

"The only ones that know my real name are those that sign my paycheck," I politely, but firmly, replied.

"Well I'm not signing anybody's paycheck, so what's your real name?" Damon asked jokingly.

We all laughed but I still didn't tell him. I just smiled at him, calling him a smartass in my head. Shortly after, we parted with 'nice meeting you' and 'have a good night.'

I couldn't get home to my bed fast enough but, for some reason; this Damon person was in my thought process. I liked his nerve of saying whatever he wanted to say. It was funny to me.

The next morning Arielle woke me up with a phone call from her apartment saying, "Giiirrrlll, someone wants to know about you and take you on a date." I was like, "Yeah, okay, whatever." She then said, "Robbie's dad called me asking about you, wanting to know if you were seeing anyone."

I was shocked because, after not telling him my name, I thought he wouldn't want to talk to me anymore. Arielle went on to say, "Damon asked me if I thought he was your type and I told him I think so."

By this time, my younger daughter, Missy, came into my room with my twins, baby girl BJ and son CJ, while Lisa was waltzing her way through my front door with my grandson. I told them about what Arielle was telling me on the phone and Missy and Lisa began to encourage me to go on the date because of what they remembered about Damon, that he was a nice man and really funny. I was hesitant and wasn't really in the mindset of dealing with anyone, let alone go on a date. I was content with taking care of my children and progressing in my career, but I was still curious about him. Arielle stated that he asked for my number and I quickly asked her if she gave it to him and she stated that she had not but asked if I wanted her to.

The girls were so adamant about it that they wore me down. I gave permission for her to give him my number and while I was anxious on the inside to talk to him, I put on a front to my kids that I wasn't interested in this man. Later that night, I received a text message from Damon asking me what I was doing. I didn't want to say that I was laying in my bed watching TV, eating cereal, with a scarf on my head, so I countered the question with the same question to him and he said he was playing spades and that I should come over. I didn't want to do that and had hoped that wasn't his idea of a date. We texted back and forth and he then asked me if I would like to go out to dinner with him. I said yes and we made plans for the following evening. Part of me was excited and another part of me was content on keeping that wall up. After texting goodnight to each other, I got out of bed to go through my closet to pull something out to wear for the following night.

2

✑

January 27, 2010
Anniversary

Then the Lord God said, "It is not good that the man should be alone; I will make him a helper fit for him."

Genesis 2:18

The next day, I kept thinking about how the date was going to turn out with Damon. I was going back and forth in my head trying to make up excuses to not go because I didn't know what to do on a date. I had been with my ex-husband for 15 years of my life and was then single from the twins' dad for about 3 years since that time. I was nervous and really didn't know what to expect. As time passed, the more scared I became. It felt like time was flying by so fast but, on the other hand, if nothing were going on, time would have been so slow.

I stopped work early, showered, primped myself and made dinner for the kids. Damon and I agreed to meet at 8PM but, unfortunately, I ran at least 10 minutes late to meet him at a restaurant called Tornado Mattie's down by the beach side. I told him what I was driving and when I pulled up, he was standing in the parking lot waiting for me. I parked and he came over to my vehicle to open my door. I could smell a scent of alcohol on his breath, but I didn't think much of it. Maybe he just took a swig

4

or two out of nervousness I thought. I apologized for being late and he assured me that it was okay and that he had not been waiting long. We walked inside and he held the door open for me.

The hostess sat us at a table by the window where we could watch the ocean and the boats. It was a nice atmosphere. Damon and I began to look at the menus. I didn't want to order anything that was overly expensive as I didn't know what his pockets looked like, so I ordered a salad and a glass of water with lemon. Besides, I made sure to eat before I left. Furthermore, I didn't know him that well to chow down in front of him. Meanwhile, Damon ordered damn near a full course meal, ate all of it with a shot of Absolut Vodka and a Heineken on the side, and started a conversation. He began by asking me what I did for a living. I told him about my foundation, my publishing company, and stated that I was also an author and had been working out of my home office since 1997. He asked what name do I sign on the books I've written and I started running off at the mouth and before I knew it, Elizabeth "Quiet Storm" Tompkins rolled right off my tongue.

We looked at each other and just laughed. He had tricked me and he tricked me good. I went on to tell him that the only people I deal with in business are the ones that knew my real name as Elizabeth Tompkins and I didn't want to tell him my name because I didn't like it. He thought it to be pretty but, for some reason, I felt like he was just saying that.

He told me about his line of work in landscaping, of which I thought was interesting because the girls told me that he actually built his pool home. He was skillful. He built houses and did the landscaping. I loved a man that worked hard with his hands. That was a real man to me, calluses and all.

During quiet moments of us eating, I would glance over at Damon hoping he wouldn't catch my eye noticing every detail of him. He had on a short-sleeved shirt with tattoos on his arms. He wore three earrings in the left side of his ear; two of them diamond hoops on the lobe and one gold ongoing hoop on the bone of his ear. I looked at his fingernails and, for a man that worked with his hands, his nails were clean. He had those hard working man hands too with the calluses on them. I loved that. Then I took a good look at his face. He was well groomed with a goatee and beautiful deep wave hair. He had one of those stern looks that made a statement of not taking shit from anybody. Damon was interesting to me, as well as cute, but I reminded myself that I wasn't going to get involved with anyone. I just wanted to stay focused on my career, take care of my children and myself.

As our evening was winding down, we finished dinner and had small talk about our ex-spouses and then our kids. We had some things in common and had some of the same thought processes regarding life in general. He was down to earth and easy to talk to. I reminded him of BJ and that the girls had told me that he used to call her his daughter and that he loved her, but he couldn't remember. *Who would have thought that several years later he and BJ would meet again and choose to call each other "Daddy and Daughter"? He was even later listed on the twins' paperwork at school as their Father...funny how things come about.*

We walked outside and I asked him if I could take a picture. He didn't know it but the girls wanted me to take one so they could see how he looked for our date. He was agreeable and I took at least two and told him that I would send them to him if he gave me his e-mail address. I told him that I would crop the pictures and he looked at me like I had just spoken in Chinese. He was like, "What is that?" I explained to him that I would cut around his picture and take out most of the background. He just laughed and said okay to be passive because I still don't think he knew what I was talking about.

Damon walked me to my truck; I gave him a hug and thanked him for dinner. He then opened my door and asked when he could see me again. I told him that I would give him a call. To be honest, I wasn't too sure if I wanted to see him again only because I didn't want to get myself into anything. I wasn't looking for a relationship at this point in my life. I just wanted a friend to hang out with every now and then. A friend only and not one with certain benefits either because that was not my style.

After pulling out of the parking lot, I called home and told the girls to put me on speaker so I could tell them how my date went. I also told them that I got his picture per their request. The first thing to come out of their mouths was, "Well, do you like him?" I told them that he seemed to be nice and funny but I didn't want to look at him like that. I just wasn't interested. I was content.

3

꧁

WHAT A NIGHT

On the first day of the week, when we were gathered together to break bread, Paul talked with them, intending to depart on the next day, and he prolonged his speech until midnight.

ACTS 20:7

Saturday afternoon, I received a text from Damon asking me how I was doing. I texted back that I was good and all was well and then asked him the same. It was text messages that went back and forth for at least 15 minutes and I tried to send him messages back that would end the conversation but he was still texting me. I yelled out to my girls that "Randy's dad keeps texting me and I want him to stop." They were like, "Mommy, NO! Be nice, he's really a nice man." I assured them that I would be nice and so I continued to respond to his text messages and finally ended it with "talk to you later," even though I really did not intend to contact him again.

Later that evening my good friend Frank called me and asked if I wanted to go dancing in Darden City because he knew of a night club that played Reggae music and he knew how much I loved to dance to Reggae. I wasn't about to turn that down so I went and we had a good time with dinner and a few of my favorite drinks, Long Island Iced Tea. He dropped me off at home around 1AM and I went to Arielle's place. She lived across the courtyard from me. She was having a party and all the kids were there along with the twins and my grandson in her bed. She had a full house.

It was typical to have a party at Arielle's on the weekend. In looking around through the crowd, the ages ranged from 21 to maybe 25. It was okay but I wanted some adult conversation and company. I needed some real grown folks and as those thoughts passed through my mind, Damon called and I asked him if he wanted to come to Arielle's place because she was having a party. He asked for directions and showed up 20 minutes later. At first, I was kind of skeptical on inviting him because of how late it was. I didn't want to appear unladylike to invite a guy out at that time of the night, but he didn't seem to mind. I met him at the elevator and there he was…bright face and smile with a scent of alcohol on his breath.

We walked into the apartment and the girls walked over to him and gave him big hugs and kisses on the cheek. Now that he had arrived, I didn't know exactly what to say to him but I needn't have worried as he started talking which made me feel a little more comfortable. I offered him a beer and when I went into the kitchen to get it, he was right on my heels. I turned around and he was almost nose-to-nose with me. I remember thinking to myself, *'ah dude, you wanna back up just a tad?'* He was like that all night. Right up on me in my face and I would just smile and remembered what the girls said about being nice to him. Maybe he was a little tipsy, I don't know, but he would talk to me so close to my face like he wanted to kiss me. I thought that's what I get for inviting a man out after hours. He probably thought I was a hoochie or something.

After awhile, I started hearing thumping noises in the hallway. It seemed that my grandson's father had come to break up my daughter's fun. He was controlling and not so nice. He was pushing her up against the wall and that was the thumping noises. I asked Damon if he heard it too and he listened closely and did. We went into the hallway and the coward pushed her again right in front of me. Damon quickly grabbed the coward, lashed out at him verbally, and pushed him down the hall to the elevator for him to leave. My daughter was crying but stated that she was okay and didn't want to have cops called or bring any attention to herself, so we all went back into the apartment and tried to enjoy ourselves again.

It was getting late and the guests were starting to leave. It had to be close to 4AM or so and Damon was still hanging around, in my face. I laughed to myself thinking, this *dude is not shy*. I didn't know what to do with him from that point on. He didn't seem like he wanted to leave, so I asked him if he wanted to come to our condo to play Wii bowling. Of course he said yes and all the kids followed. That was the only reason why I invited him to the house because I knew my kids were right behind me, as well as some of their friends. He sat on the couch and watched the twins play while I got comfortable into some sweatpants and a flannel shirt. If he was gonna like me, then he was gonna like me just as I was dressed up or dressed down. I really didn't care how he felt about my appearance at this point anyway because I was still not interested in him like that.

I sat next to him on the couch and BJ squeezed her little bottom in between us and rested her head on his arm. They took to each other quickly. He then put his arm around her and kissed her on the forehead. The first thing I thought was, 'wow my man is really laying it on thick with the kids.'

Amidst of all the noise from the game and the talking from my girls and their friends, I kept hearing the thumping noises again. I went out into the hallway and went to Lisa's door, as she lived in the condo down the hallway next to mine. I put my ear up to her door and I heard arguing and my grandson crying. I went back to my place and told my other girls and their friends to come with me in case I had to beat that coward's ass and everyone knows how I am about my kids, but I had to be careful because of my foundation, a nonprofit against domestic violence. They came with me and we banged on the door until Lisa answered and I sped past her right dead in that coward's face, touching nose to nose, forehead to forehead, begging him to put his hands on me, calling him every name in the book. The girls' guy friends stepped in between us, moved me out of the way, and got in his face. I noticed my baby girl walking in and I was trying to make her go back home and then here came Damon. He picked her up and took her back to my place and gave me a look of "come on."

I followed him and promptly called the police and once they arrived, I explained what the problem was and they made the coward leave for the night. Lisa was so upset; she didn't want to press charges, she just wanted to go to bed. After the girls' friends left, Missy stated that she was hungry and Damon agreed that he was too and suggested we all go out to Henry's to eat. I told him that I was in my comfortable clothes and, besides, it was almost 5 o'clock in the morning. None of them seemed to care at all. We all fit in his well-kept Cadillac and headed out. I couldn't believe this man paid for everyone. There were seven of us and he allowed everyone to order what they wanted. I gave the girls a look of "you know what to do" and that meant, you don't order anything expensive and not a lot. They did just that.

As everyone was talking and eating, I noticed Damon staring at me while Missy was in his ear going on and on about nothing. He was conversing with her but still staring at me. The way the two of them chatted you would have thought they had known each other since birth. I remember thinking, what in the hell could they be talking about, they have only known him for three years and it wasn't like they saw him every single day. When Damon got up to take the twins to the 'grab a stuffed animal machine', Missy looked at me and said, "Awww...Mommy, he's cute."

"I know, I can see that, but I'm still not interested."

I was afraid of getting hurt. Don't get me wrong, I enjoyed a lot about Damon already. For one, I loved the fact that he was an older man. He and my kids got along wonderfully. That was a plus by itself. He and I shared the same views on parenting and about life in general. That was easy to work with. We both had been through abandonment in regards to our spouses and we were both hard working individuals. We understood working hard and taking care of a home, but I still was not interested. I was content and at peace with my life.

Damon took care of the bill, drove us home and walked us to the door. I gave him another hug and thanked him. I also apologized about what happened with Lisa, but he laughed it off and said, "Your family is just as crazy as mine." Even though he seemed cool about it, I still didn't think I would ever see him again. He was just letting me down easy.

4

∝

THE TEST

That each one of you know how to control his own body in holiness and honor.

1 THESSALONIANS 4:4

Since that night, surprisingly, I did hear back from Damon. We would send text messages back and forth. I wanted to make it up to him with having dealt with our family issues and spending his money on everyone, I wanted to have him over to watch a movie with me. I had a free night without any kids, the twins were spending the night at Arielle's place and Missy was spending the night at her friends' house.

Damon knocked on the door around 9PM. I had on lingerie on purpose with candles lit, light jazz in the background and the TV on ready to order a movie. He came in, gave me a hug and we walked back to my bedroom. I dressed like this, setting the atmosphere this way on purpose in order to see if he would act like a dog or not and to see whether or not he would go for it. That would determine whether I would leave him alone completely. I had to see if he was a real brotha or not.

We ordered a movie, although I can't remember which one it was, and tried to agree on what to eat, as he didn't eat red meat or pork. I sat on the bed and got under the covers. He lay on top of the covers, on his back, at the bottom of my bed with his arms folded under his head. We stayed this way until the movie was over. He started getting sleepy and so was I so he got up, came over to me, gave me a kiss on the cheek and a hug. I tugged on his shirt a little to pull him closer to me to receive a longer kiss from him. He was receptive, but resistant. He gave me the longer kiss but stated that he should go.

In my book, he was a keeper. I liked that about him. He wasn't only after one thing from me or he would have done so that night. If my plan had backfired, I had a back up to say that I was on my period. He was a gentleman and I enjoyed that about him too. He was a grown man and not a dog, an older man that I always desired. His actions made me want to ease down that wall and open up to him more and I did just that. I told him about my 3 month county jail time in California at the hands of my father and brother.

My story was that, before my father had left for Israel, I had gone through a divorce and times were hard for my kids and I. I asked my Dad if I could use his social security number to get gas turned on in my house and he agreed and gave me his information. Shortly thereafter he left town. I did not utilize the information until almost a year later. My brother made a call and pretended to be my father and got the gas turned on in our father's name. Well time went by and I couldn't afford the bill and when I moved to Florida, my brother moved in with me along with his entire family. I soon realized that they were using me and no one was helping me with the bills or food and our kids were in constant arguments. They were all Jehovah's Witnesses and we were not and that was conflict by itself. I asked them to leave and my brother's revenge against me was calling the California Police, pretending to be our father, and had charges pressed stating that I used his name illegally and when my lawyer finally got in touch with my father, my father stated that, yes, he gave me permission but that he no longer cared that I was in jail because he was upset that I let the gas bill go to collections. I since wrote a book about that called, "Jailed By Blood: Inmate 798175."

When I told Damon my story, he was very understanding and never judged me. That was all I needed because that part of my life was devastating and he took it all in and didn't walk away. He then began telling me his jail stories, but he has since gotten his record expunged. Since that night, I thought about how all of my guy friends were respectful to me and we could lie on my bed and watch TV and no one would even think of making a move. I wanted to add Damon to my collection but, for some reason, I wanted to put him in a glass box and place him on a shelf...I wanted to know him.

5

The Invite

So God created man in his own image, in the image of God he created him; male and female he created them.

Genesis 1:27

As time went by, Damon and I would text and call one another. We were getting along pretty good. One evening while I was just sitting around with him on my mind and a text message popped up asking, "What are you doing?" I replied with, "Nothing, I was just thinking about you." He suggested I come over to shoot a game of pool and have a few drinks with him and his other roommate, Hank. I was so glad he asked. I wanted to be in his presence. I couldn't wait to see him. I informed Missy of where I was going and she was all smiles and said, "Ooohhh you go boo!" We laughed and I headed out to the liquor store to grab a bottle of wine. I didn't want to show up at his house for the first time empty handed.

I followed his directions to his home and when I pulled up in the driveway, I must have fixed my face a thousand times before getting out of the car, checking my nose, my hair, and when I finally got out of the car, I started checking my clothes like I had OCD–obsessive compulsive disorder. I was just nervous. I mean, I was going to a man's house by myself after not dating for about 3 years.

I shut the car door and began walking up the walkway and rung the doorbell. I remember thinking to myself just before my finger hit that bell, *'oh boy, no turning back now.'* He answered with a pool stick in his hand and a big smile on his face that made me smile even wider. He gave me a hug and a kiss on the cheek and I handed him the bottle of wine. He had me follow him to the kitchen where he placed the wine in a cooler and he took out a huge wine glass, rinsed it out and placed it in the freezer. He said it was for me. That was a new one on me with the chilling of the wine glass. The small things drew me nearer to him. That was like *'old school stuff'* to me. I was fascinated by him and his *'older man ways with all the old Motown music he would play.'*

Damon introduced me to Hank as *"his Baby."* Hank put his hand out for me to shake and looked at Damon with an approving nod of his head. Damon went on to tell Hank that I wrote books for a living. Hank began asking me what types of books and I told him that I wrote true stories, nonfiction, but that I published other authors who wrote in other genres such as Christian, fiction, and so on. The atmosphere seemed pretty relaxed and calm.

Damon poured the wine into the chilled glass from the freezer and I sat on the bar stool next to the pool table area and watched them play. Damon was a pro, but you would often hear him say, "Oh I'm not that good, haven't played in a long time," but it was obvious he was an excellent player. After getting his butt whooped twice in a row, Hank handed me his pool stick and asked if I wanted to play. That took me by surprise because I just wanted to sit back and watch and was way too shy to play with them, especially against Damon. Just as I was forming my mouth to say no, they both said, "Awww come on, it's just pool." I didn't want to seem like a sourpuss, so I grabbed the stick and told them that I didn't want to embarrass them or anything with my skills and we all laughed. I then embarrassed myself because I only made like 4 of my balls while Damon finished the game with the eight ball.

It was fun. I had not enjoyed myself like that in a very long time and I loved being with Damon. His spirit was calm and his aura was on point. He was relaxed and made me feel the same. I caught myself stealing peeks at him but when I would sneak a peek he was already looking at me. I quickly put my head down with a smile on my face. Then he sat down on the couch next to me and his face was even closer to my face than the night we had a party at Arielle's place. He just stared at me and smiled and I did the same. That moment of silence said a lot in our smiles and staring into each others eyes.

6

⚸

PARTY HOUSE

*Above all, keep loving one another earnestly, since love covers a multitude
of sins. Show hospitality to one another without grumbling.
As each has received a gift, use it to serve one another, as good stewards of
God's varied grace.*

1 PETER 4:8

It seems like Damon's doorbell was always ringing. He kept company
and there was always a house party going on that consisted of music, spade playing, alcohol, food, and just laughter and camaraderie.
I would often wonder how he could get up for work so early at 5:30AM
after staying up drinking so late into the wee hours. However, he did it.
Breaking our moment of silence was Aaron announcing that the doorbell
ringers were Adam and Levi. Damon whispered in my ear that he consid-
ered them to be his sons. He would refer to a lot of the younger males that
he was in contact with as his sons, even Aaron. He also told me that Adam
and Levi were both gay. I never would have guessed from the way they
were dressed. They looked like tough guys, especially Levi. He sported a
doo rag with a ball cap on top and a pair of dark sunglasses and they both
would wear their pants sagging. Damon introduced us and they came off
nice and shook my hand. I noticed that Levi was a bit nonchalant, but
Adam was friendlier.

During interaction as the night went on, Adam would randomly say, "Oh my God, you are so pretty and so nice," and would give me the biggest hug. I loved that he was so receptive of me. He made me smile and I would embrace his affection and acceptance towards me. He made me feel so comfortable. Moments later the doorbell rang again, this time it was his actual son, Robbie, and his friends that showed up. I couldn't tell you how many there were but they all went out back on the patio by the pool.

In being observant in my surroundings, all I could think about was having my girls with me. It was like they were my protection. I didn't like big crowds, especially in a house. It wasn't safe to me, plus I didn't know anyone there except for Robbie and Damon. It's not that everyone wasn't nice; I just started feeling out of place because there were no other women there but me. I looked at the clock on the microwave and it was just a little after 11PM. I noticed Damon out back with the others and I stood in the kitchen looking out at him, wanting him to feel me as I didn't want to interrupt him talking, hoping he would catch my eye and he did. He came in and asked, "You okay Baby?" I told him that I was fine but that it was getting late and I thought that I should head on home. He walked me to the door and out to my truck, ending with giving me a hug. Again, he was so close to my face like he wanted to kiss me, so I kissed him on the cheek and said that I would talk to him later.

Driving away, all I could think about was Damon. I was getting weak for him in such a short amount of time. I was battling within myself to go with the flow or stop it before it got started. It felt good to have the feelings I embraced in such a short period of time, but that feeling could also be harmful. I just wanted to live and be happy. I went with the feeling and my heart took over my mind and both were on the same page. I liked this man and wanted to be 'his Baby' and was especially happy with the fact that he was an older man.

Day by day, communications grew stronger between us. We were now a good three months into our relationship. It was on an almost daily basis that I was over at his house. It got to the point that he wanted me to bring all the kids over too and when I did, the girls and I would cook for him and everyone else or he would cook for all of us. He just loved family he said. My own thoughts were that he missed the family life he had with his ex-wife and the atmosphere. I could certainly understand that. I did as well when I was with my ex-husband.

Quite often the kids and I would go to Damon's house, as would Adam, Levi, their Mother, Audrey, Aaron, Jason, and Robbie, of course, with a few of his friends. It was a loving environment and everyone took to each other as though we were all family. We had music in the background with a card game of spades and others shooting pool. Damon would often cook, as well as made sure I had a chilled glass of wine. It was fun, food, drinks, family and friends almost every night of the week and when the weekend came, it was the same version of the week before.

7

⤏

TRUST ME

It is better to take refuge in the Lord than to trust in man.

PSALM 118:8

Damon introduced me to one of his friends, Brenda. Brenda was a friend of an old ex-buddy of Damon's. She was an African, tall, dark-skinned woman that had to have stood at least 6 feet tall. She wore those shiny black short hairstyle wigs that fit her head like a cap along with dark sunglasses because the circles around her eyes were darker than her dark skin tone.

Damon would tell me stories of how he and Brenda would travel a lot together. When I met her, she seemed okay, couldn't really establish anything with her as far as her personality, but I did sense bougieness. Whenever she came over and I was there, just Damon and I, she would give me looks as if to say, "hmmph!!" with her nose turned up at me. I wanted to make sure that was what I saw, so I just kept it to myself for awhile but she would do it every time whenever she came to visit. In front of Damon, she was "oh hey, how are you?" with a fake smile, but as soon as he turned his back, it was back to the "hmmph!s!" again while looking me up and down. I didn't know what this woman's problem was. From Damon's take about her, she was only a friend to him and nothing more. They never had sexual relations or even kissed, strictly friends, but you wouldn't believe it judging by her actions towards me.

I wanted to tell Damon what Brenda was doing but how could I tell him and be assured that he would believe me? I mean, he knew her way before he knew me. Then I thought, well, I am his girlfriend and if anything, he will hear me out and understand my feelings. I just didn't want to seem like drama to him but a few more of her evil eyes and "hmmph!s!" with the turned up nose at me; it was going to get ugly real fast. I kept my cool though and kept it to myself, as Damon always spoke highly of her so, how could I tell him she was being an ass to me and he believe me? So to keep the peace, I said nothing at all. He already seemed to take offense when I whispered to him of how tall she was. I guess to him it was like I was talking negatively about her but I wasn't. He looked at me with a firm look and said, "She's a good friend and a nice person," and then he walked away. I didn't mean to offend Damon about his friend, but seeing that I must have from that small comment, I knew that there was no way I could tell him how she was toward me when he would leave the room.

She didn't stay for long whenever she visited if it was just he and I, but when she did visit, they would always go to the back patio to chat about trips they went on previously and about the trip they had planned before he and I got together. There was nothing I could say about that. It was previously planned and from the sound of it, they were definitely going. I dreaded that of course, but had to eat it. When she left, Damon would walk her out to her car and she would walk past me without saying a word. He seemed to act differently whenever she was around. He wasn't as loving toward me or silly acting. He was more serious and acted like he didn't know how to act when she was there. After seeing her off, he came back inside being the person he was before she came. *(Damon was always so good to me when it was just he and I. He was very attentive and we would chat about anything and everything).* He was back to calling me 'Baby', hugging and kissing me, being sweet and loving again, so I had to ask.

"Damon, is there something or was there ever anything between you and Brenda?" I inquired.

"Baabby, noooo! I told you she and I are just friends. Nothing else, I promise you that. Have I had opportunity to sleep with Brenda? Yes I did. Did I want to, no I didn't. We are only friends and if you're worried about our trip coming up don't because there's nothing to worry about okay?" he explained.

"Okay. I believe you and thank you for not getting mad when I asked you about it."

"No, I like that you asked me and didn't accuse me."

He made me feel comfortable and secure. I was satisfied and happy.

The weeks were winding down and it was time for them to take their trip, a long ass week trip in another state to enjoy scenery, shows and gambling. Oh God I couldn't stand it! I trusted Damon but Brenda's actions made me second guess everything he told me. His actions, as well, bothered me since he was being so standoffish towards me whenever she came around and she always managed to come when it was just he and I, as if she scouted his place to see what cars were in his driveway. I helped Damon pack several suits and his necessities because he was leaving the next day but I didn't want him to leave without becoming one with him. I wanted to indulge in his essence before taking flight so I initiated an intimate encounter. In fact, that was our first intimate night spent together since our three month courtship. He made me feel beautiful, wanted and loved.

Morning came and Damon was gone. He texted me just before he got on the plane to let me know that he would have to turn his cell phone off until they were actually in the air. I appreciated his communication and every effort he was making to contact me during his trip. He would text me when they landed and even gave me a few phone calls. Every day that he was gone he would send me a text to say good morning and goodnight. I think they had a few more days left on their trip and Damon actually told me that he loved me and missed me. I kept that text for a long, long time, as I kept going back to it just to read it over and over again. It made my heart happy and overwhelmed. He actually said it first and it didn't matter to me that it was in a text. He said what he felt in his heart towards me. He also stated that he was ready to come home to me and to see everyone. He wanted me to send his love to them all. I assured him that I would. I made plans to make a huge dinner for him and all our kids and friends as a welcome home gift. I couldn't wait to see him. I needed to feel him. Embrace him. Inhale him.

Changes started to come about in Damon's household after his return. We would still have our nightly gatherings with family and friends and, at times, it would be just us along with his 2nd roommate, Hank, and his new girl, Amanda.

Amanda was a tall awkward looking girl with long brown hair. She appeared to talk through her nose. She was a bit of a lush too and it didn't take much for her to get drunk but she could shoot a good game of pool. She and I had taken to each other pretty well in a short period of time. We became so close that we began to hangout together without the boys and chit chat over the phone if we weren't meeting up at Damon's. One night in particular, Damon didn't call me and when I called him, he was short with me and acted as if he didn't want to be bothered. It was obvious he didn't want my company so I stayed away. *(I soon learned that starting an argument with me was something that he would often do when he wanted to push me away to be with another woman.)* I remember lying in my bed that night around 1AM; I was woken up with a gut hurdling, heart drenching feeling inside. Almost like my feelings were hurt and torn up. It made me feel like something wasn't right somewhere with someone so I began placing my kids one by one through my thought process and with each one individually, that feeling eased down, then I tried my mom and the feeling was the same as the kids, then I tried Damon and there it was. The feeling came back upon me stronger than ever. The first thing to pop in my mind was that he was cheating on me. Around this time, if we didn't sleep over each other's homes, we would text one another because we couldn't sleep no matter what time it was – 2AM, 4AM. I texted him and he did not respond. I called him and it went straight to voicemail. I started to cry and Brenda entered my mind as who he was cheating on me with.

Later that morning I received a phone call from Damon and I informed him of my call to him and he said his phone must have died. I asked him if I could come over to see him and he said that I could. I couldn't get there fast enough. When I did, Hank, Aaron and their friend Jason were there. I pulled up and Aaron and Jason were standing out in the driveway talking, looking at me strange like they knew something. I jokingly said to them, "I know ya'll was hanging out last night." Jason just smiled at me and Aaron said, "Yeah we were out, cuz we didn't have company last night." I thought to myself, what in the hell does that mean? I walked inside the house and Hank gave me a hug and said Damon was upstairs.

I went upstairs calling Damon's name and he looked exhausted with a T-shirt and jeans on, lying across the bottom of his unmade ruffled up bed. I stopped in my tracks and stared at him and that feeling returned stronger than ever before and my heart started pounding profusely. I asked him if he had cheated on me last night and he said yes that he had and motioned his arm toward the bathroom and said for me to clean out my drawer because it was over between us. I cried a damn river and started pulling the sheets off the bed that I had just bought the day before with him still laying on them that eventually made him fall down to the floor and he started to laugh. I didn't understand him at all. "WHY?!!! WHY?!!! WHY?!!!" I screamed to him over and over again. He stayed silent and couldn't look me in the face. My heart was so weary and my body felt weak. This was the reason I hadn't wanted to let my guard down. This was the reason I didn't want a relationship with anyone. This was the reason I stayed alone and buried myself in work and took care of my kids. I dreaded this very thing that was so familiar to me after my 15-year abusive marriage and my 3-year devastating emotionally abusive engagement to the twins' dad...hurt. I didn't want feelings like that to resurface but it did and it hit hard with a ferocious force. What I spent years of removing made a home in my person...again.

He grabbed a grocery store bag and tried to help me put my extra toothbrush, hairbrush and clothing into it and I snatched it away and filled it up myself with blinding tears filling my eyes, rolling down my face like a faucet. He knew of my past. Why did he do this to me was my question to myself and God while packing my belongings. I began to walk out his bedroom door but not before grabbing the bed sheets and placing them into his trash can outside. Making my way through, Hank looked at me and said for me to stay strong.

Damon went outside on his back patio by his bedroom and I yelled up to him while vigorously throwing my stuff into my truck.

"I hate you! You ain't shit and that's why you're going to die an old, bitter, lonely, mean ass old man!"

Still not being able to look at me, he slowly lit a cigarette, looked out towards the tall trees across from his home, blew out a puff of smoke and said, "I don't hate you and you will always be 'L' to me."

'L was short for Love, which was his nickname for me.' I got into my truck and sped off recklessly. I can't even put into words how I felt at that moment as the pain was so intense times infinity. As I am writing this, I still cannot describe it. I allowed myself to love this man and his return to me was to show me disrespect and disregard. I went home and all my kids were at my house. I couldn't hide my face. They always greeted me at the door when they would hear my key and when they saw me; they quickly asked, "Awww, Mommy what's wrong? What happened?"

I couldn't even talk from crying so much. We had a period of silence as they settled for giving me love and affection and then hugging me tightly until I muttered, "He cheated on me."

"What?! With who? Do you know?" Lisa asked.

"I'm not sure, but I think it was that Brenda chick," I replied.

"Oh that bitch gotta go! Where does she live?" she asked.

We all started laughing and I was snottin' at the same time. It was nice to have my girls with me. They always made me feel protected. Each one had a piece of me in them. Arielle was my Spirit, Lisa was my Strength, and Missy was my Soul.

"Damon needs his ass kicked too!" said Lisa. We all agreed to that.

"And big bird, ugly ass (pertaining to Brenda) is gonna get it! You know we can do a drive by," Lisa insisted. "I can't believe Damon climbed that big ass mountain." She had us laughing again because Brenda was at least 6 feet tall with that amazon build look and Damon was only 5 foot 3 inches.

"Did you fight him?" Lisa asked.

"No girl, I was too upset. I wanted to but my hurt feelings got the best of me," I replied.

"Oh he doesn't know you yet. He hasn't even scratched the surface," Lisa stated.

"No he hasn't, but I've got a feeling he will. Let him keep fuckin' around and he'll see and then we'll be like, MAMA NO!!" said Missy.

"We can do a drive by and throw those little green Bibles at his house if you want to," added Arielle.

We all laughed our asses off. They made me feel so much better, but the hurt was still in my heart, just not as intense. We then began to back track to when he didn't answer his phone, trying to piece everything together. It was only making me angrier because it made us think that he was cheating with her for the duration of their trip and her ignorant ways towards me was jealousy because she felt like I was invading her territory... Damon.

I then received a phone call from Amanda, letting me know that mine and the girls' thought process was all wrong after I told her what happened. It wasn't Brenda who Damon cheated on me with, it was Chelsey. An ugly, bad body ho that everybody had per Amanda, from Orville Heights about 20 minutes away. She said that Hank was telling her that she was Damon's "white girl." The girls told me to not contact him again and to just ignore him if he was to call or text me. I told them I wouldn't, but my heart silently said I would answer if he contacted me and he did.

A few days later Damon sent me a text message asking if we could meet somewhere to talk. I texted back asking where and he said the park. I told the girls that I was going to get some air, but I know they knew I was full of shit.

I met Damon at the park and we began to take a walk. He started off with saying he was sorry. I asked him if he loved the person he slept with and he stated that he did not, but he did like her. He said she was just someone he messed around with from time to time, but there was nothing serious going on between them. He also stated that there were 'others' that he had been having sexual relations with, but he wasn't serious about anyone. I asked him if he knew the dangerous position he had placed me in with sleeping with 'others' and he apologized again, but that wasn't good enough. He stated that he understood if I didn't want to see him again, but he would like for us to give it another try.

"You don't have to answer now, but please think about it," said Damon.

"What are you planning on doing with your 'others' Damon?" I asked.

"The others and I will never happen again. I felt at the time that I didn't want a relationship with anyone, but I care a lot about you and I want to be with you, so please just think about it and let me know. No pressure. I don't want to lose you 'L,'" he said.

We hugged and he kissed me on the cheek and we parted. At this point, I didn't know what to think. I mean, I loved Damon and I wanted more than anything to be with him. I wanted to forgive him, but if we got back together, what would the girls say and think? I hoped they would understand because my heart was considering it, but my mind was not agreeing. It was that battle again just like in the beginning before we started dating. I was thinking and I was thinking hard. I wanted to be happy again and being with Damon made me happy. In just being in his presence in that short period of time took me from the feeling of never smiling again. I went home and told the girls that Damon and I were getting back together. They looked at me and said they wanted me to be happy, but to be careful. *'Words I should have lived by.'*

8

⋊⋉

APRIL 27, 2010

But when Herod's birthday came, the daughter of Herodias danced before the company and pleased Herod.

MATTHEW 14:6

Serious changes took place in Damon's household as Hank skipped out on him without paying two month's worth of rent. Hank owed at least $800 and left while Damon was at work. He tried many times to contact Hank, but he wouldn't return his phone calls. That left a bad taste in Damon's mouth and he vowed to not look for another roommate. With his birthday just around the corner, I wanted to do something special for him. I got on the Internet and started looking up jazz clubs and restaurants. I had a poem that I wrote for him and wanted to recite it with jazz music playing softly in the background. I found a really nice spot in Johnsville. It was a bit expensive but, hey, it was my love's birthday and I wanted it to be a night he would not forget.

I went to his house dressed in a black and burgundy ribbed cut dress with my hair done in an updo hairstyle. He left the door unlocked for me and I went upstairs to his room while he was getting dressed in nice black slacks, with a button down shirt and diamond cuff links. He looked so handsome. I sat on his bed and noticed a bottle of Absolut Vodka beside his file cabinet. He had two shot glasses and said to take a shot with him

25

before we left. What should have been one shot was actually two for me because it was so strong. I had to chase it with the Heineken beer he had sitting on his night table. When he took his shot, it was like water to him. He made no face and didn't need a chaser and took another shot.

I told him that I had a surprise for him and I hoped that he was going to like it and he smiled and said, in a mumbled voice, "Don't be giving me no G**damn surprises!" *He always joked like that.*

I hated when he would curse God or use His name in vain and he would do that quite often and every time he did, I would quickly say a prayer under my breath of *'God please forgive him and have mercy on his soul.'* Damon would always mumble something negative whenever I talked or presented something positive to him or for him, which to me; it meant he really enjoyed it. *Like I said, he was always joking, which meant he didn't like the mushy stuff.* I never paid his negative mumbling any mind. It was funny to me.

While Damon was completing his attire by putting on his Stacy Adams, his cell phone rang. From the sound of the loud voice on the other end, it was Brenda wishing him a happy birthday and wanted to take him out, but he politely told her that he was going to dinner after thanking her for his birthday wish. What bothered me was that he didn't tell her who he was going to dinner with. *Whenever she would call and he and I were alone, he would never say he was with me, he would just say, he was relaxing or watching a movie or eating dinner when he would be doing all those things with me.* I think she knew it was with me though because her voice downplayed from loud to low. *I could feel her looking me up and down through the phone with an hmmph!! under her breath.* It was a short conversation. I didn't want her ignorance controlling my emotions, so I blew it off and asked Damon if he was ready to go.

On our way out the door he asked me to leave my truck in his garage while we switched vehicles and I drove us in his Cadillac to our destination. I couldn't wait for him to see the surprise I had. We communicated en route and talked about how we were not going to argue about anything, as it seemed like small things would make Damon angry fast. At times, I didn't know what I could say or couldn't say. I would be too nervous to just speak my mind right out; I would ponder things over in my head before allowing my words to escape my mouth regarding my thoughts. *I had to do this when he was sober because he had quite a temper that eased up just a tad when he would drink. Although drinking made him more laid back, if he had too much to drink, which would be all the time, he would be right out mean if he didn't go to sleep. Instead of drinking in moderation, he drank to get drunk. Oftentimes, he was a happy drunk that kept you laughing and somewhat of a functional alcoholic because no matter how much he drank, he always got up at 5:30AM and went to work everyday.*

Upon arrival at the restaurant, part of the highway was under construction and it was hard to get to where we needed to go. I was trying to follow the pattern, but ended up having to make a U-turn and, needless to say, this didn't make Damon too happy. He started shaking his head from side to side and yelling at me to pay attention to the road, of which I was, it was just complicated with detour signs and one ways. I realized I hated driving with him on the passenger side. Finally, I detoured to a side street that took us into the lot of the restaurant. I quickly found a parking space so I could get out of the car as soon as possible just to 'woosah' under my breath. I had to save myself so to speak. After shutting the car door, we were half way to the restaurant entrance when he asked me if I had locked the car up. Why oh why did I forget to do that? I said no and sorry while clicking the button at the same time to lock up the car and gave a smile just to ease the tension that has so quickly formed. I wanted so much for him to enjoy his birthday with me, as it was our first birthday together during our relationship. I didn't want us to be mad or arguing with each other. I wanted peace and a good night. I wanted us to be happy.

After being seated, he joked about seeing his ex-wife inside the restaurant. I played it off and gave a fake smile and laugh and followed it up by suggesting that if he saw her, then we should invite her to have dinner with us. *Damon's story was that his ex-wife of 20 years left him once, but never stated why, but elaborated on it the last time she left him for good. She also took the majority of their furniture, left bills on top of bills and made no effort to contact him again, as did one of their sons who made the decision to reside with his mother. His son had also stolen from him as well, per Damon. He had stolen personal items along with money. Damon was very troubled about the matter and felt anger towards that son.* After I made my comeback remark about seeing her, he preceded to go toward the restaurant door to get her. We just laughed it off.

From where we were seated, we couldn't see the live jazz entertainment very well so we requested a seat closer to the front. I needed for us to be close to the front anyway so I wouldn't have far to walk onto the stage to recite my poem for him. I informed the host that it was Damon's birthday and that my poem was my other gift to him and I wished to have their soft jazz playing in the background. They loved the gesture and granted me my wish. After we ate our dinner of what I vaguely recall as being chicken linguine fettuccine served with a double serving of both Absolut and Heineken for him and my favorite Long Island Iced Tea for me, the announcement of 'Happy Birthday Damon' came over the microphone and took him by total and complete surprise because his cute little face turned red as a beet. He just stared at me with a grin. Then the host introduced me on the stage as Quiet Storm. Just before I started, I let the crowd know, as well as Damon, that '*I call him King because he treats me like a Queen*'. They didn't know he was just being an ass to me in the car. All you heard was the crowd say, "awwww." This was Damon's first time hearing me call him by the nickname I birthed in his honor. My words were a flow of:

KING

I listen when you speak and I hear the silent cries as I gaze into your eyes.

I realize the pain consumed in your heart as you part from a reminiscence of your past that seems to be hidden in your present.

I am your here and now, the future in your life, I am ready to be a soldier and stand by your side in turmoil and strife.

We gain strength through Christ and turn a house into a home. I give you my shoulder to lean on. Be the backbone to your front bone and together we stand strong.

I assure you, you will never be alone, as we journey through life's ups and downs and turnarounds taking the bitter with the sweet.

I bathe in the promise of my bonded word that your history will not repeat.

Allow positive speaking to manifest and run deep and embrace the words that are leaked.

And so on, and so on, we move on with black strength and black pride.

From the knowledge of our power bestowed upon us from heaven up above.

King we are blessed and when I look at you...I see love.

He had never heard me or seen me perform before and I must say that he now appeared to be very impressed judging by the look on his face. At one point, I saw his jaw drop. It made me feel good to know that he enjoyed my gift to him. The crowd gave a huge applause, but all I saw walking off stage was King's red face and bright smile. People started walking up to him, telling him happy birthday. One sweet looking caucasian old lady of about 80 came over to him and slapped him a high five and said '*you must be something pretty special.*' He was so flattered and couldn't stop smiling. Once we had our time back to each other, King leaned over to me and said laughing, "I'm gonna kick your ass," and we both laughed so hard. I told him, "your welcome." I knew he loved it. He kept looking at me smiling in between sips of his Heineken. He admitted that he never had anyone do anything like that for him before and that made me feel even better to know that I gave him a memory of me on his birthday.

After dinner, we hit the liquor store to get a bottle of Absolut, a 12-

pack of Heineken, and a bottle of White Zinfandel for me, another one of my favorite drinks. I had to laugh because we didn't go inside to the liquor store; it was actually a drive thru. I thought that was so damn ghetto. I have never seen anything like that before. I just wanted to get back to Lake Shores fast before it got any later. While driving, I reminisced to myself of the drive there and I didn't want that to happen again so I prayed in my head for God to please let us make it home safe and without conflict. He heard my prayer. We got to King's house and told Aaron about our evening and shortly after, called it a night and we had a nightcap.

9

Jekyll and Hyde

Rendering service with a good will as to the Lord and not to man.

Ephesians 6:7

King and I began to ride a rocky roller coaster ride on a daily basis. He made me feel like I couldn't do anything right. I pissed him off with every little thing. Either I was too helpful or I was too nice and I don't know when that became a problem for anyone to have someone treat them like a human being. I was me. I didn't know any other way to be unless I allowed you to take me out of character. I refused to allow King to do that because I knew that once out of character, I was a pistol. I didn't want him to see that side of me. Every time he was negative toward me, I tried harder to counter it with positivity by saying, let's just sit down and talk to each other, but it never worked. Somehow, we got on this unhealthy and ridiculous routine of whenever King felt like we were spending too much time together, he would be mean to me, say ignorant things on purpose to push me away so he could do his dirt and I would go with an argument. A day or so later, he would call or text and ask what was I doing and wanted to know if we could talk. I always responded by meeting him somewhere or just going over to his house. I just wanted to be in his presence. When I arrived, he would put out another shot glass for me, as he had already had a few and tell me, "Take a shot nigga, you need to catch up." We would cheer our glasses and swish it down, but I had to have my chaser of either beer or wine to deal with the taste.

While there, I would notice him looking at me sideways like he was angry with me about something, but would never say. It felt like he was just going over whatever that look was toward me through his mind. I didn't know what to think or what it could have been. *Did he have a bad day at work?* I asked him what was wrong and instead of saying nothing like normal people, he always had to snap with a smart ass remark like, "Did I say there was something wrong?" "Did you hear me say anything was wrong?" I would try to bypass the tension in the air by saying, "Okay, so there's nothing wrong," and then tried to follow it up with asking him how his day was to take him out of his weird zone.

He would never tell me about his day. He would always act like it was a top secret thing to share. I tried sharing with him about my day and share good news about my foundation or my publishing company and he would stop me and say *"if I didn't ask you, then I don't want to hear about it"*. He never wanted to hear about my day or any good news I would have. Needless to say, he would ignore that question about his day and start doing laundry and I would turn on the TV and have his dog, Spike, sit next to me on the couch. Speaking of laundry, that was another thing. He folded his clothing a certain way that was mixed with military style and department store ways, as he used to work in a men's clothing store many years back and was an ex Navy man. He dumped a basketful of clean laundry onto the couch, looked at me and said, "Come on nigga, laundry folding 101."

He would be joking, but serious at the same time. First was the shirt. You had to lay it out straight and flat with the back of it facing you. Then, you would pull the right side of the shirt over to the middle with the arm slightly folded back to the corner and the same for the left side. Flip the bottom up toward the middle twice and flip over and it's done. Boxers were folded twice and flipped downward. Socks were folded over once, never to be placed inside each other like a ball, as it will stretch the sock per him. If there were booty socks, you don't fold them, you just lay one on top of the other. Pants, mostly work jeans, line up the inseam and fold over once and work shorts are not to be folded at all, just line up the inseam. It took me several tries and some deep sighs from him before I got the shirt folding right. Apparently, he wanted me to learn this. Then when it was time to make the bed, I had to make sure it was even on both sides and fold the corners at the bottom of the bed before tucking underneath the mattress and you couldn't just stuff it, you had to swoop it quickly in order to achieve that tight fit per him. There's nothing wrong with being neat, I'm neat and King has taught me something and now, my lil' ones and I fold our laundry the same way and make our beds the same way.

Shortly after, I started having nightcaps at his house on a daily basis.

I would get up in the morning with him at 5:30AM and always hear him mumble *'aww shit, shit, shit!'* I would began to iron his clothes while he shit, showered and shaved, as he called it, and I had to be sure that he had a crease in his work jeans. I made the mistake of not making a crease one day and you would have thought I burned a hole in his pants. Then came a smart ass remark of "who taught you how to iron?!" I just ignored him, re-ironed his jeans with the crease and with starch as requested and took my shower. I knew my mouth and it was too damn early.

'During school days, after leaving out when Damon left, which was around 6:30AM, I would go home to catch 30 minutes of sleep, then get up with the twins to get them ready for school if Arielle was still asleep and get them off to school at 8AM. Then my work day began at 9AM.' Mornings were always those 'eggshell' moments that I was careful of with Damon. I made sure to not say too much because I didn't know who I was waking up to...Jekyll or Hyde? So I would wait for him to speak to get a feel of his demeanor then follow suit. When I first started staying nights, I remember making the mistake of trying to hug him before he got up, one and two, talking. All I talked about was what my day was going to consist of. Guess he didn't want to hear it and he would lean down to my face as I was sitting on the bed and hand me the remote with a mean look as if someone pissed in his Cheerios and mumble, 'news, channel 13.' That remote handing came along with a hard stern look. I learned that morning. He shut me up without saying too much of anything.

After departing and going our separate ways, at any point during the mid morning hours, I would randomly receive a text from him thanking me for *all that you do,* i.e., keeping the kitchen clean, helping with laundry, and ironing his clothes, buying him cigarettes, vodka, beer, and/or take him lunch except on Fridays if the barbeque man showed up. I would wait for at least 10 minutes before I responded because I felt like I had to be careful in what to say. I didn't want to say too much nor could I just say your welcome or what? This was so damn stupid. I just texted back, *your so welcome* and put a smiley face at the end. I think even that was too much for him. He didn't like a lot of 'nice' things to be done for him and it seemed like the nicer I was to him, the shittier he was to me. If I was mean in response, then he treated me a little bit better. To me that meant, I had to step out of character to be respected by this man, but that didn't always work either. It was damn if I do and damn if I don't.

He didn't like my kindness; he said I was too nice. I started coming back in response to his smart ass comments and he would say I was a nasty mother fucker. This was all starting to get old, but not soon enough. My nature has always been that of a 'ride or die' that often worked against me. Not good. Not good at all.

10

✄

THE SETUP

A false witness will not go unpunished, and he who breathes out lies will not escape.

PROVERBS 19:5

Since King's birthday fell on a weekday, Brenda decided that she wanted to throw him a birthday party at his house. She knew that I had already taken him out for dinner for his actual birthday earlier that week but she acted like we were in competition. I know she was just doing this to spite me and who in the hell throws a party for someone at the house of whom the party is for? Wouldn't you throw it at the house of the one who was planning the party? At this time in our relationship, he and I were still rocky. Some days he would talk to me and most days, he didn't. When I would catch him on the phone, his tone was like I was annoying him and he would rush me off. I understand if I called him while at work, but this would be well after when he was home. I wasn't going over there much because of his attitude, so I didn't dare just pop up. I didn't know why he was acting like this towards me and if I asked if everything was all right, that would have been an argument by itself, so I ate it. I ate a lot of his shit to avoid conflict, but conflict still occurred.

Surprisingly, later that day, I received a call from King and he was in good spirits.

"Hey, Brenda just called and said you were invited to the birthday party she is throwing for me at my house."

"Oh really?...okay what day exactly and time?" I asked.

"Tomorrow night around 7PM. She really wants you to come and I think you should," he said.

"Okay, I will be there."

After I hung up with him, I sat at my desk pissed off. What the hell did she mean I am invited to my boyfriend's house for a party she was throwing for him and why doesn't he see anything wrong with it? Exactly what was going on here? I told my girls, they felt that I shouldn't go, but I was adamant about attending, so they let me know that I was not going by myself. We had my mother watch the twins and my grandson for the weekend while we went shopping and got our hair done. The girls made sure that I looked better than ever.

Saturday night and my heart was beating a thousand beats per minute. I was so damn nervous. We pulled up to his house and had to park on the grass across the street because Brenda's car was parked right next to his in the driveway, as if she had been there for awhile along with a bunch of other cars parked in front of the driveway and along the grass in front of his house, left and right. He had an extremely full house. We parked and the girls reminded me to be nice and to not let Brenda make me mad. I promised I would be on my best behavior.

The music was loud and the door was unlocked so we walked in and Brenda was the first face we saw. She came in from the back patio smiling until she saw all of us come into the kitchen with a bottle of wine and her smile went away quick with a look of disappointment and anger at the same time as if to say *'damn!'* She did not want us there and the atmosphere was strange. There were so many white people there, which wasn't a problem, but they all were in a huddle with King and Brenda joined in chatting away like no one else was around. The only ones that were familiar to me were Jason, Robbie, Audrey and her ex-husband. I went over to King and poked him in the back to not interrupt him so much and he looked half way over toward me, but not looking at me, and said so coldly, *'Hey how you doing?'* and then he turned back to his conversation. I didn't understand why he was acting like that. I looked at the girls and they motioned for me to come into the living room where no one was and suggested that we leave because he treated them the same way when they spoke to him. He would usually hug them with a squeeze and call them Baby with a kiss on the cheek, but he didn't know any of us this night.

I told them that I wanted to stay until he talked to me like he had sense. I wanted an explanation. They hung around and we went into the pool table area where he broke from his conversation and began shooting pool with this young looking white girl that looked to not even be 21, but the way she talked, you would think she was 12. She said, 'hey Daddy would you like me to get you a beer?' and King responded, 'yes, please Baby, thank you.' WOW! We all looked at each other with our mouths open and he continued to play like we weren't there. Then another white girl that looked to be just about 21 came over to him and said, 'Daddy give me the keys to your truck, we'll be right back' referring to her and her friends and he handed the keys over without a blink of an eye and a smile on his face, 'here you go Baby.' Then the *'12-year-old'* came back with his beer and said with a laugh, 'oh what can I say, that's just Daddy' because he shot a ball in the corner pocket and Missy got pissed and snapped with, 'oh, I know Daddy very well thank you.' We were all pissed and the girls had had enough. They insisted I go with them but I wasn't going to leave without talking to him first. I told them to take my truck and go home because I planned on staying the night. They didn't think it was such a good idea but they went and didn't bother to say goodbye to King and just walked out. A few minutes later Brenda took me by the hand and asked if she could talk to me outside for a minute.

I was nice and I let her hold my hand while we went out front down the walkway and just then, the girls slowed up, stopped the truck, and Lisa and Missy came over to us and just listened to make sure Brenda wasn't talking shit to me and after they saw her smile and hold both my hands in front of her, they walked away, got back in the truck and left. Brenda's daughter continued to stand behind the front door listening.

"Storm, listen, Damon told me that you ask him a lot of questions about he and I and I want you to know that there is nothing between us. We are just friends. I love him and he loves me like brother and sister and that is it. Nothing else." *At this time, I was pissed that he even told her what our supposedly private conversations were.*

"He and I go on a lot of trips together but as friends and that's it. He is going through a lot because of his separation and I just want him to be with someone that is going to be good to him."

"But…" I tried to interrupt.

"Storm…he loves you. He does. He is just trying to give you a hard time on purpose to see if you will stick around. He told me about you buying him clothes and taking him lunch. I know you love him too. It's okay. Don't let him get to you. Let's go back in and have a drink that I made in the blender and let's have a good time."

"Okay…okay," I said.

Then she gave me a hug and we walked inside and the tall, giant silhouette at the door tried to disappear, not doing a very good job. I walked in feeling a little bit better until he continued to ignore me; then the feeling sunk right back into my heart again. I just stood up against the deep freezer looking and feeling out of place. He even had the audacity to toast champagne with Brenda and gave her a peck on the lips and hug in front of me, then to top it all off, he turned on the TV, turned the music off and put in a video of their Vegas trip they took a month back showing them taping each other while at dinner, at shows, and at the hotel as if they were a couple and you could see the looks from the guests that they were confused. They then looked at me as if to say, "I thought you were his girlfriend" or "I'm sorry," while the ones that didn't know what was going on praised them and laughed with them, asking them about their trip and than all I saw was Brenda and King looking at each other with a devilish grin on their faces, then look over at me. I fought back tears that tore my throat up. *What was his reasoning behind this? Why did they want to embarrass me and hurt me? I didn't even know her and why would he do this to me and allow someone to do this to me? I was beyond hurt. I was more than devastated. I was dying where I stood and even though I was in a room full of people...I felt so alone.*

It was getting late and everyone started taking plates and heading out and he kept the video up, but turned down the volume, while I brushed passed him and went into the area where the pool table was and started shooting pool by myself. I was hoping he would come in and talk to me, but he didn't. Instead, he made fun of me to Brenda and the others that stayed behind of whom I knew and started running behind Spike like he was picking up his dog shit, insinuating he was me, placing the shit in his pockets saying, *'oh don't worry, I'll clean it up'* and they all started laughing and the loudest one was Brenda of course.

Shortly after that, Brenda began to pack up plates and headed out saying she would see him tomorrow to clean up. He walked her to the door and Audrey, her ex, Jason's friend James and I were the only ones left. I was still in the pool room and King came in and shut the lights off on me, said *time to go* and walked away. Everyone had a puzzled look on their face and asked him if everything was okay and he seemed angry and said he was leaving so everyone had to go. Audrey quickly hid his keys because she knew he had been drinking, but he raised so much hell about having his keys returned that she gave them back to him. We all started walking out and I was followed behind him and he got into his truck and shut his door and locked it. I knocked on his window and gave him a little smile.

"Hey, open the door. What's wrong?" I inquired.

"I don't like when people talk shit about me to other people at their houses!" he snapped.

"WHAT? What are you talking about?"

"You know what I'm talking about!"

"I don't know what you're talking about, please open the door and talk to me."

"Take your ass home!"

"I can't, the girls took the truck and they're already gone. How am I supposed to get home?"

"Find a way!"

Why did he say it to me like that? Like he was blowing me off and then he waved his hand off to me as if to say get away. Nothing pisses me off more than to have someone blow me off like I'm less than nothing. I hit his truck window with my fist and he jumped out, grabbed me, and pushed me up against his garage door. Jason and James grabbed hold of him and I got into my boxing stance and told them to let him go. I started walking up on him and capped him in the jaw and then he tapped me on my forehead. We danced down the driveway out into the street while screaming obscenities to each other. I kept my boxing stance the whole time and then went into kickboxing mode. His eyes got so big, and then he suddenly started to laugh. That made me even madder. I rushed him, started punching him in his ribs, grabbed hold of his waist, swung him around and threw him down on the ground and jumped back into my stance. He laughed even harder. After that, Jason and James were standing beside us whereas King was across from me and James was on my left and Jason was on my right and when King came towards me to hit me, they stopped him, but when I went towards him to hit him, they let me go. Aaron came from nowhere and stood in between us.

"What the fuck are you doing?" Aaron asked King.

"Stay the fuck out of it. We're playing!" King responded.

"She don't look like she playing to me."

"I said stay the fuck out of it. What are you doing, taking her side now?! You gonna go live with her?" King yelled.

Aaron walked away but the other two stayed in position. King and I kept going at it and they continued to do the same thing for when he came after me, they stopped him, but when I came after him, they let me go as if they wanted to see me kick his ass. Audrey kept trying to grab hold of my arm yelling for me to stop. While in motion, I yelled back to Audrey that he was talking too much shit. She continued to yell and at one point grabbed my arm, but I was too rough and broke away from her and went back to him because he kept running off at the mouth calling me out my name and aggravating me on purpose all while laughing. Then I noticed his face getting serious when Robbie came out with his girlfriend and Robbie was yelling at us to stop fighting. King seemed to grow balls when Robbie came around and acted like he wanted to fight me for real so I got back into kickboxing mode and when he came toward me, I threw a kick

37

at him, almost hitting his face every time to keep him from connecting.

Audrey grabbed me one last time and pulled me into the car with her and her ex-husband and we drove off with King still taunting me at the car looking into the window where I was seated in the back. I waited to break-down after we drove away. I apologized to Audrey and told her I never come out of character like that and that I didn't know why he treated me the way he had and she assured me all was okay and no need to apologize because her and her ex have been through it before. She said she under-stood. I heard her ex say, *'she's good'* in regards to my fighting. The rest of the car ride home was in silence while I pondered through my thoughts of how Brenda and King set me up. I also felt that this was the one time I didn't want my girls around because I didn't want them to see me fighting. They heard stories of me beating ass, but never saw and I wanted to keep it that way. They dropped me off and all my kids were at home along with some of their friends and they asked me what happened at the end of the night and I told them. Their friends thought I was cool and Missy added, "Told you my mom was gangsta!" We all laughed and I demonstrated how the fight went. I told them that Robbie's girlfriend tried to jump in to take up for King and they didn't like that at all. They vowed to kick her ass if they ever saw her again.

For some reason, I started feeling good inside. I don't know if it was because the fighting allowed for the frustration of the night to let out or because I knew I beat his ass. The girls asked me if I was okay and I told them how I was feeling and they felt that as long as I was fine, then all was good. I told them that one thing for sure; it was over between us because I knew he would never contact me again. Not a woman that beat his ass. I went to bed that night with a smile on my face, running back the fighting session. However, I was still puzzled as to what he was talking about when he said I talked about him. I had no idea and at that moment, didn't care anymore. I kicked that nigga's ass in front of his friends and in front of his own house.

11

⚮

TRUTH

For the wrath of God is revealed from heaven against all ungodliness and
unrighteousness of men, who by their unrighteousness suppress the truth.

ROMANS 1:18

It wasn't even a full 24 hours before I received a call from King. I didn't
answer of course. He had to be crazy to call me after what just took
place. Since I didn't answer him, he sent me many text messages asking
if we could talk and that there was something he needed to tell me. He was
begging me to please answer him that it was very important. I ignored
both text and calls. I didn't trust him. I even thought that he would try
to get me to come to his house so he could call the cops or press charges
on me or something. I mean, it sounds stupid now, but at the time, things
were so intense and crazy, I didn't put anything past him anymore. My
trust in him left the night he cheated on me, but it left completely with this
incident. At this moment, he was a liar, cheater, and fake. Someone that I
knew would never have my back. After not answering him at all, I received
a call from Adam. I answered and Adam asked me if I was okay and before
he could finish any other words, I hear 'L Baby, please talk to me...' and
I hung up. I didn't want to hear anything he had to say. Then I got upset
with Adam because I know he knew what happened less than 24 hours
ago. Adam texted me later on that day, saying that King had snatched the

phone away from him but I didn't buy that.

Almost a week went by of King calling and texting me and I didn't answer him. My mind and heart were in a good place. I wasn't hurt anymore and I wasn't upset. I was good. Really good and had no problem with moving on. Then he called Arielle asking her to please have me call him. This man actually went through my kids to try to contact me. When Arielle told me about him calling and texting her to relay messages to me, I decided to get in touch with him so he would stop contacting her. I sent him a text that read *You no longer exist. 'Ur dead 2me! Never contact me or my kids again!'* That text did not matter to him because he continued to text me and call me. Receiving a text from me after a week seemed to have made him call and text me even more. He sent one last text that read *'L, I'm sorry Baby. Things went too far that night. Please talk to me and let me explain.'* I then called him and he asked me to meet him at the park. I agreed because I wanted to know what he meant when he said I talked about him at people's houses. That sounded so silly to me. Who told him something like that? I was about to find out.

When I arrived, he was sitting in his truck. He got out and thanked me for meeting me. I didn't want to hear all that, so I firmly asked him what he was talking about when he said I talked about him. He went onto say that Brenda informed him that I went to his ex-buddy's house and talked shit about him to the ex-friend and his wife. *Now I knew what he was talking about.* Only thing is it wasn't King that I was speaking of and I never went to the house to do it. The wife of his ex-friend was the principal to my twins and her and I became close and shared a lot of our personal business. The principal confided in me that her husband was cheating on her for quite some time now, but she didn't know whom with, but I did.

Back when I asked King if he was cheating on me with Brenda, he let me know that I was wrong in my thinking but that she was having an affair with his ex-friend for years and still to this day and one of the reasons why he and the ex-buddy are no longer friends is because the ex-buddy felt like King took Brenda away from him after he introduced them. *(This was something King always did; he would get the number to his friends' girlfriends and ex-girlfriends and have the girls' hangout with him if they were broken up.)* For that to be one of the reasons for them not to be speaking sounded childish and petty, but it goes much deeper than that as far as the damaging friendship they have. I was told, however, the kicker is that Brenda had been a married woman for years at that time, married to a wealthy 80-year-old, white man. She was taking both the ex-buddy and King on trips. Her husband had no clue as to what type of wife Brenda was to him but soon found out because he had recently left her. When Brenda found out that I told the principal about the affair she was having with the principal's husband, she told King that I went to their house and told his business about what was going on inside his house. She played us against each other and now she no longer speaks to King at the request of the ex-buddy that she is still having an affair with. In passing, I can still see her as she gives me evil looks and makes the stupid *'hmmph!!'* sound at me. I just look at her and laugh because she's an ass and I was upset with King at that time because of how he went by what she said and not ask me anything. That entire night was unnecessary and caused a lot of hurt and horrible embedded memories. That night is when I began to look at him sideways with no trust and when my feelings and love toward him began to fade.

A man who views the world the same at fifty as he did at twenty has wasted thirty years of his life.

Muhammad Ali

12

✤

TAKEN FOR GRANTED

And as you wish that others would do to you, do so to them.

LUKE 6:31

Months had gone by with King and I being off and on. Reasons being, whenever he wanted to *'have his time away from me'* he would start a no nonsense argument about something so small and turn it into something so big. I would call and text him, but he would not respond during those times. This would be after a few days or so, and then he would tell people that I was crazy and a nasty muthafucker, which was why *(his version)* we fell out at the time. He only told people about my reaction towards him after he would do something ignorant or disrespectful to me *(like the time I threw a rock through his bedroom window for not answering his door for me. The reason for that anger outrage was because he pissed me off for trying to hook up with my girlfriend's sister that was visiting out of town and my girlfriend brought her over from my invitation to his house to eat crab legs with us and play spades and all was great until they started playing footsy under the table, then his many comments of changing her last name to his and making her daughter his daughter and having a bedroom for the daughter and burying money in his backyard with their names on it, then to top it off, they tried to exchange phone numbers before Arielle caught them.)* He never told what he did to me to make me react out of character toward him. He never told the truth. He always pointed the finger to me and never took the blame for anything, especially when he was wrong, which was 90% of the time. Not that I was perfect, but I didn't do ignorant shit to him on purpose or treat him bad. I was good to him and everybody knew it, including him. I did for him like any other woman would do for a man that she loved. I took care of him in more ways than one and not just sexual. If he needed, he knew he could depend on me whether it was running errands for him to pay a bill when he couldn't because of having to be at work, whereas I worked from home, so I could take a break and handle his business if I didn't have a meeting to attend.

I would share dinner with him when I made dinner for my kids and take him a plate so he wouldn't have to worry about cooking when he got off work or he would just come over after work when I would text him what we were having for dinner. He would have a beer and a tiny pint of vodka waiting on him, and then we would all watch a movie. If his funds were low, I would keep him supplied in cigarettes, beer and vodka. I would take him lunch on a daily basis while at work, help him clean his house by sweeping while he mopped, did dishes, folded laundry, helped mow the lawn, and decorated his place. He gave me the money to purchase contemporary art-work that he admired in my home and I hung curtains in his place at my expense, decorated the guest bathroom with a throw rug and matching face towel set and purchased glassware sets to add to his collection. There was nothing I wouldn't do for him. (I knew that none of the trash he messed around with or planned on messing with wouldn't do any of that. The only other person I knew of that would wash and fold his laundry, and keep his house clean was Levi. He occupied King's house for three weeks straight after meeting him at McDuff's.)

There were several occasions where King would cancel out on me to watch a lifetime movie or America's Next Top Model with Levi. The atmosphere and the demeanors began to change as well whenever I would come to King's house and Levi was always there, but he was not too friendly toward me anymore. My girls began to notice it too. It was like he would get upset and make an excuse to leave. It concerned me, especially since one of my daughters asked to use Levi's cell phone and he gave her permission. After making a call she needed to make, Levi was in the bathroom so she looked through his phone and found King's number saved in Levi's cell as "King Boa" and text messages between the two of them back and forth of sexual remarks to one another. There was one where Levi told King, 'I did what you asked me to do (meaning Levi talked to me for King to get me to come back over to his house after we had an argument about Brenda...this was some-thing I noticed he always had Levi do was talk to me for King and calling me odd hours of the night until he did exactly what King told him to do) now it's time for you to pay up' Levi continued in his text message to King, 'are you ready for me? I'm at your bedroom door'. This text was sent to King at 7:30 in the morning. I confided in Amanda and asked her if she thought King went both ways because whenever he got drunk, he would consistently talk about how he would screw other men and mentioned about how he actually had screwed other men when he was in jail for three months in his past. I then told about how I would sleep in the nude and if I tried to touch him, he would grab my hand and tell me to stop or pretend that his shoulder would be hurting.

She laughed and tried to convince me otherwise. Months later, I received a text message from Levi after King and I began to get more serious. (Yes I stayed because I loved him unconditionally.) The message read:

"Love hard, but be careful and follow your heart. I will tell you why later." I texted back, "'Huh?" However, Levi would not reply nor would he respond to any of my calls so I informed King of the text and he snapped at me and said to delete it. I asked him what was going on and if I could help with anything and he yelled, "I got myself into this and I will get myself out of it! You can't fix everything so stop trying! I will talk to you later!" and he hung up on me.

I told Amanda everything because we could talk about personal things like that with the trust that it was only between the two of us. However, shortly afterwards, I found out that Amanda told King and Levi that I said they were sleeping together. When I tried to defend myself, it was too late, no one believed me, but I always knew that the truth would come to light. Amanda and I fell out because of the lying and as time went by, Amanda and King cut ties as well. Per Amanda 'King allowed two, in her words, "nigger black bitches" beat her ass while she and King were hanging out at a local bar. King was a nigger from her mouth to his ears.

Levi stopped speaking to me for almost 2 years after the text message he sent me until just recently. *He said the past was the past and that he and I were okay.* I was good to King. My heart wasn't hard to see nor my feelings for him. Just like people could see how good I treated him, they could see how bad he treated me, but they would never say anything. Instead, they would go along with him and condone his bullshit ways. Everything was so damn funny. He liked the attention and they enjoyed giving it to him just to watch him act a fool, especially when he was drunk. They weren't his friends. He was being used and for some reason, I think King knew this, but felt like he needed people around him to keep from being alone with his thoughts, his past, himself. They were using him and he was using me emotionally because I was stronger than he was mind-wise when it came to dealing with the past. He knew I didn't like seeing him hurt. He knew I would always be there for him no matter what. He knew I was always there for him...ride or die. Most of all, he knew I loved him...he took me for granted.

13

☙

PLAYGROUND

Do not be deceived: "Bad company ruins good morals."

1 CORINTHIANS 15:33

It never failed. King always had a houseful of guests, the ones from our circle and several new people that he just met from allowing Jason to bring with him, which were always young white girls on a daily basis. King and I were at least 20 years older than everyone and even more than 20 years older than the strangers that he allowed to get comfortable, as some of them were under 21. It was a revolving door and I wouldn't get a call until well after midnight to come over to his house to chill with him. When I walked in, I saw a drunken young white girl walk out behind Jason. I always told King that he needed to be careful because he didn't know who the parents were of any of the young girls Jason would bring to his house and he didn't know if they were telling the truth about their age with allowing them to drink in his house.

Strolling through the kitchen, I bypassed different brands of alcohol along with cases of beer and going a little further to the back patio, some of the girls were dressed in bikinis. I would get pissed to see this because I would wonder how long this party was going on before he called me to come over. That's why he would say come straight upstairs. I was not to go through the house, but I did anyway. It was ridiculous to see this beautiful

46

home turned into a whorehouse and he allowed it. One drunken young white girl stumbled up to me and warned me to not get into the Jacuzzi because Jason had just fucked a girl in it. People were so drunk; they had to stay overnight and some of the young white girls stayed in the bedrooms with the guys, even during his work week because it was a constant party each day of the week.

I remember getting up with him one morning and we went downstairs to do our routine of filling up Spike's food tray, opening the blinds in the family room and in the kitchen and turning on the news. The kitchen was so disgusting with shot glasses, empty beer bottles and empty vodka bottles covering the kitchen island and kitchen table. Takeout food leftover containers was not put away, and the waste basket was overflowing. There were ashes on the kitchen table, the floor was scuffed up with black marks and there was a sink full of dirty dishes. People were laying on the couches, snoring from the living room to the family room. King never said a word, he just took his 9 different vitamins from the cupboard like he did every morning with a glass of juice, grabbed whatever he could find for breakfast and walked past everything and everyone as if he didn't smell the stench in the air or hear the snoring.

His place was used as the younger circles' playground. They disrespected his house the way they did because they knew they couldn't get away with it at their parents' home and they wouldn't disrespect their parents in that manner, but King allowed it at his house…anything went. He allowed it because they needed a place to go and he didn't want to be lonely.

Once they departed his house, they went to their own homes. He always stayed too drunk to realize that he was actually being disrespected and used. I would witness them stealing his cigarettes, then turn right around and ask him if they could have one. Of course, he would give it. This made me keep his cigarettes in my purse to keep them from stealing from him. King had to ask me for one of his own cigarettes to smoke. Then they would go to the vodka (*of which a majority of the time either he or I would buy and no one else ever pitched in or went to purchase more and the same was also truth with regards to the food. He would throw money away and just spend on anyone and everyone whenever he got drunk.*) When he would keep the vodka in the refrigerator, we began noticing that it was getting lower and lower day by day but then magically fill back up inch by inch because water was being added to it. (*He eventually started keeping the vodka in his bedroom.*) Others would borrow money from him with a promise of paying it back, but never did per King and I'm not talking about chump change either of $5 or $20, it was always like $100 or more. I even witnessed grocery shopping take place in his own house whereas they would get an old grocery store bag that King would keep on the floor of the pantry and they would commence to take snacks from the pantry, then hit the fridge and make sandwiches and not just one or two. Before you knew it, they would leave his house with either one full bag of groceries or, at times, two full bags.

I would notice King leaving his wallet lying around on top of the deep freezer by his lunch box. I would put it in my purse and take both my purse and his wallet and lock them in his bedroom until we went upstairs to bed and then handed him his wallet the following morning. When he got drunk, he was more careless and that's why I felt like I had no other choice but to watch out for him.

I would also hear the company talk shit about him saying "that little nigga is drunk as fuck" and "that short midget muthafucker is crazy" and "that muthafucker is stupid." They didn't know I was listening. I wanted to tell them to leave, but what could I do? It wasn't my house and he and I were not meshed in that way where I could put someone out of his house. I would stand by his side with one of my hands holding him behind his back and the other hand holding his left hand just in case he staggered a bit too much and that way I would be able to catch him should he stumble. Then he would whisper to me, *"Baby, I'm really drunk."* He would then wipe the top of his head with both hands and slide them down to his face. I would continue to hold him up because of his staggering. It was like he didn't know when enough was enough.

At times, I would walk King upstairs to his bed and leave everyone with Aaron, assured that he would lock the house up. I wouldn't go to sleep until every car was out of the driveway and then, after I heard Aaron come upstairs to his bedroom, I would sneak back downstairs to go behind him to make sure that the house had been locked up and, sometimes, I would start to clean up if Aaron hadn't gotten it all.

Now I had my shared moments of being drunk myself don't get me wrong, but when I would realize that King had more to drink than I did, I would start to drink water to sober up so I could watch out for him. I felt like I had to do this especially if we had 'new' company in the house. They all would look at me like I was the 'party pooper' and would state to me that I wasn't his mother and he wasn't my child and I wasn't his wife. That much was true, but he was my love and being in the state of mind that he was in, I was not going to let them take advantage of him, not on my watch. That's when they would convince him, as well as influence him, to go out with them without me. *(Trouble always surfaced whenever these certain people were around. I wasn't the only one that noticed either. It was brought to my attention by several of the others in our circle. No one really liked them and they always stirred up drama, but King didn't care, he would help with the drama. When they came around, people greeted them but then they would disperse. I, too, wanted to do the same but, unfortunately, I also wanted to keep the peace going between King and I so I would remain silent and just watched and listened to the 'kids' for half the night.)*

When I tried to tell King what I felt and what was going on, he would just argue with me and that made it even worse between us, which in turn made him want to leave me and go out with them even more so and that led up to us having bad arguments, fist fights and he would often come home with less money. It got to the point that he would spend nights at the younger circles' homes in another city. God only knows what went on then, but I had a pretty good idea as they had no respect for me as his woman in my presence because they would point out other women to him just to watch his reaction and he would give them a show. I was so tired of the disrespect from them and from King as he would never have my back when they would be asses to me. He would just laugh along with them and add to it. *(They didn't know that he would apologize to me later. This is something he would always do, yell at me to try to belittle me in front of these kids and talk shit about me to them like he didn't give a damn about me, but after they were gone, he would say he was sorry and then show me love and affection, such childish bullshit).* Those nights everyone thought he was so damn funny. He wasn't funny…he was just drunk.

14

ॐ

TRAGEDY

He heals the brokenhearted and binds up their wounds.

PSALM 147:3

A week went by with King and I not speaking. I think that was the longest period of time that we ever went. Normally, it would be like one to two days. I tried to keep myself busy with working out (kickboxing and jogging) to not think about him but it was hard. I often wondered what he was doing, who he was with, what he was thinking and if he was thinking about me. I hated that I loved him like I did because he didn't hesitate to give me his ass to kiss whenever he wanted to push me away. Even though we had some bad times and even terrible times, all of our times together were not awful. When I say that, I mean that when he and I were alone, either out to eat, shopping, *(King would take me shopping randomly or just hand me $100 to shop for myself because he knew I never took that kind of "me" time and if I needed, he would provide, especially for the children)* or just watching a movie spending quality time together, he was more than wonderful to me when it was just us. We even took random trips to Tampa to gamble, we went to NFL football games, and UFC and MMA fights. Those times are what I was holding onto. Those times were what I cherished and what made it harder for me to remove myself from him completely.

We would do things for each other and never had a problem spending on each other. I was holding onto the moments that played a serious part on my emotions and that was not good for me at all. Suddenly breaking up my thoughts of him was a text I received from Jason asking me what I was doing and how was I doing. *(See, this was routine with us. Whenever King and I were arguing, he would have either Aaron or Jason watch my social media page to keep up with my statuses because he and I were not friends on there at the time or he would have them text me to see what I was up to for him instead of him contacting me himself. Even after I caught on that this was what was going on, I continued to play along as King would always say, 'throw a dog a bone' and I did just that and threw his words back at him without him realizing it.)* I told Jason that I was doing great, keeping my head in my work, taking care of myself and going to the gym. Naturally I was lying to him as I was actually sitting in my room and sulking over King. But, after I told Jason that, he texted back, and told me that he had to go. It was so obvious that he had been checking up on me for King.

Even though King was nearly constantly in my thought process, I still didn't want to see him. I was trying to break away from him for good but every time I tried, the harder he would push. I was just so tired of going up and down on that emotional rollercoaster I allowed him to lead me on. It was game playing after game playing and, yes, I still loved him, but his meanness, mistreatment, cheating and disrespectful ways toward me were diminishing my feelings for him. I realized that I couldn't make him love me. Hell, I questioned if he even truly liked me. I would tell him, "I love you" and I didn't hear it in return, only if he was drunk, which wasn't too often, not the being drunk part, but saying "I love you" part. He would take me by surprise if he ever said it to me first when semi-sober, or randomly give me a hug and kiss in the morning and just squeeze me tight, but he would always follow it up with, 'you will never hear that again or you will never get that hug and kiss again.' He would be joking when he would say that according to him, but it was hard at times to determine if he was serious or not. It got to the point where I didn't expect anything good as far as words from him and I stopped altogether telling him that I loved him. I would just say it in my head. Twenty minutes later, Jason once again texted me, reminding me that it was his birthday. I wished him a happy birthday and told him I had a gift for him. He said he was going to come see me but I knew that King would be in that visit in some kind of way so I told him that I would meet him at Wilson's Supermarket instead.

Later that evening, as I was heading out to meet Jason, I received a call from King. I knew it!

"Hello?" I hesitantly answered with an attitude.

"Where are you L Baby?" he asked.

"I'm gonna meet Jason to give him the birthday gift I have for him" I replied.

"I know Baby, but I don't see you, I had to come here to get a few cleaning items for the house." He lied.

I pulled up to the front and there they were, Jason with a smile on his face and Barbara, Jason's girlfriend of five years—*a sweet young lady that was truly a pillar in the community. She was a member of the National Honors Society, was attending college and placed on the Dean's List multiple times. She worked at a local grocery store as an Administrative Coordinator and volunteered with one of the police department's P.A.L. program. She was drawn to Jason just as much as I was to King and whenever and whatever Jason wanted or needed, Barbara provided without hesitation.* Jason and Barbara walked up to my vehicle and he reached in first and I gave him a hug and kiss on the cheek through the window, handed over his gift and I then gave Barbara a hug and kiss on the cheek and complimented them both on how nice they looked. I asked Barbara what their plans were for the evening and she stated that they were going out to dinner and before I could finish my conversation, 'hey Baby' comes from the right side of me.

"I don't care if you're mad at me, you're still my Baby," and he then rushes a quick kiss on my lips and smiled. I just looked at him and turned my attention back to Jason and Barbara and told them to have fun. I drove off wiping my mouth thinking about King. I was mad that he kissed me because I didn't know where his lips had been since we hadn't spoken to each other in a week and he smelled like alcohol already. I went home and watched TV until I dozed off but was awakened by my cell phone ringing around 4:30AM, it was King. For him to call me at that time, I knew something was wrong.

"Are you okay? What's wrong?" I nervously asked.

"There was an accident Baby…Jason is in the hospital in bad condition and 'B' passed," he said with sorrow in his voice. I was silent for a moment.

"Barbara is dead?"

"Yes."

"WHAT?! What happened? Where are you? I'm coming to you guys?"

"NO! Don't come. I can't handle that right now. I only called you because you're the closest one to me and I don't want you to see me like this," he explained.

"I'm coming to the hospital. I want to be there for Jason."

"Please just listen to me and don't come. I'm about to leave. I will call you later today."

I tried calling him back but he had turned his phone off. I then called Arielle and Lisa and informed them of what I was just told. It was unbelievable and such a hard pill to swallow. I just saw them earlier that day, how could something like this happen so suddenly? With all of us on the phone, we began to talk about what could have happened and wanted answers. We knew exactly who to ask…Aaron. He was always telling and blurting things out without knowing he's giving information.

Lisa called Aaron and asked him what happened and he told her they were all at King's house and Jason and Barbara were tired of waiting on King to get ready upstairs so they went ahead to a restaurant in a nearby city where they were all going to meet up at and he rode along with Jason. *(Now there is one thing that I know…King will not drive to another city with alcohol in his system by himself for fear of a DUI. He would either have Aaron as his driver or me and since he and I was buggin' and Aaron was with Jason and Barbara, who was his driver because he was already tipsy earlier that day when I met them at the supermarket?)*

Lisa asked him who was with Damon and Aaron kept saying his cousin. That 'cousin' was always a lie coming from Aaron because everyone was his 'cousin' and with Lisa knowing Aaron as long as she has known him, she knew he was lying and covering up for Damon and suggested that the 'cousin' was a woman Damon had with him and that's why he didn't want me to come to the hospital. She hung up with him and called me and told me something wasn't right. I then called Aaron myself.

"Hey Baby, are you okay?"

"Yeah, just hard to believe this shit really happened. I mean, you know 'B', she was a good girl. Man this is fucked up!"

"I know Baby…still can't believe it myself. I wanted to come to the hospital but King wouldn't let me, then he turned his phone off and I don't understand why. I mean I know we were buggin' but damn, look at the circumstances. What happened exactly?"

"Well, we were leaving the restaurant and Jason and 'B' were in her car behind us. I was driving Damon's truck."

"Were you all racing or what?"

"Yeah…I, I…I mean no. We were just far ahead of them and then we didn't see their car headlights anymore and Damon said to turn around. I turned around and drove back to look for them and they both were on the ground. Jason tried to get up to look for 'B' but Damon told him to stay down because his shoulder blade was sticking out of his neck and my 'cousin' found 'B' and she said she had a pulse."

"I know everyone was devastated. How is your 'cousin', is she okay?"

"Yeah, she's all right. She was crying and everything."

"Well, I'm gonna go Baby. You get some rest and I'm gonna call you later today after I go to the hospital and, hopefully, the doctors will let me see Jason."

Later that morning, I called the hospital and asked what room Jason was in while I was en route to the hospital. They connected me to his room and his mother, Tonya, answered. I introduced myself to her and informed her of how I knew Jason. Tonya stated that they were about to transfer Jason to another hospital in a different city because he had to undergo surgery and then she told me which hospital he would be going to. We quickly exchanged telephone numbers so she could keep me posted.

Since Jason was being transferred, I decided to pay King a visit. I pulled up to the grass on the side of his house because I noticed that a beat up, white truck was in his driveway. Suspecting someone was with him, I called his cell.

"Hello," he answered whispering.

"Bring your fuckin' ass down here now or I'm coming up those muthafuckin' steps and I will really raise some hell!"

"Hello," he answered whispering yet again.

"Bring your fuckin' ass down here now or I'm coming up those muthafuckin' steps and the I will really raise some hell!"

I was more than heated. I was so heated; I scratched an "X" on the passenger side of his caddy, his pride and joy, to get back at him. *(He didn't realize it until a few days later.)* He came outside and couldn't look me in the face and kept his head looking down at the ground. I wanted him to give me back some items of mine I had been storing in his garage. I really wanted him to look me in the face, but he couldn't. I remembered looking at him wanting to smack the shit out of him. He knew all the time that he was going to be with someone else that night when he kissed me at the supermarket, making it sound like he still cared about me. Yes, I was jealous, hurt, angry and sad at the same time. My emotions were truly mixed up.

I blamed King at first regarding the accident because I couldn't help feeling like he should have acted like an adult in the situation by stopping them from leaving the restaurant that night and, why in heaven did he allow them to race on top of that? But I knew it wasn't King's fault and I was upset with the fact that he had brought someone into our circle just a week after we argued. He had only known this person for one week and, already, she was lying on my side of the bed, as I always called it.

I still loved him and still wanted to be with him, I had just wanted a week's time of being away from each other to think about what we needed to do to make things better between us and, instead, he went out and slept with someone else, but was texting me like he was thinking about me. That was the kind of stuff that I was talking about. He didn't think…he just acted and when he did think, it was always with the wrong head. Then after he was done whoring around, he wanted to drown me with bullshit lies of how much he missed me and wanted to be with me to get me back, but then the cycle would repeat all over again. It was an unhealthy rollercoaster ride and that needed to be fixed, but he wasn't willing to work on it.

I left after I retrieved my belongings, gathered my kids and we all went to the hospital to see Jason. When we arrived at the hospital, we looked for Jason's mother. I had never had the pleasure of meeting her so I looked for a woman that looked just like him and that was almost everyone there, as they were all family. I had to inquire with a gentleman at the desk to point out who she was. She was a young looking mother and looked like she didn't take any shit. The girls and I went over to her and I reintroduced myself and we gave her a hug, then we waved at his father who looked like he could have been Jason's brother. *King often joked about Jason's father looking younger than Jason was and he wasn't lying. I had to laugh to myself when I saw him.* It had to have been at least 30 minutes later and King, Aaron and a woman that was with King showed up. Aaron saw the girls and me first and looked back at King and his guest to inform him that we were there. King kept his head down and didn't even look at us. The girls caught him by surprise and gave all three of them a hug, not knowing who she was, but it didn't take long for us to figure it out.

We began to talk amongst ourselves via text messaging and thought that maybe she was Aaron's grandmother because she looked that old, even older than King with thick glasses, tits that hung down to her stomach, more gut than ass, and she was dressed with high water jeans, some kind of blouse that had a vest made into it, and what looked like orthopedic sneakers. Her hair was of coarse texture in a ponytail hairpiece that was of fine texture sitting on top of her head. Most of the text messages consisted of *"LMAO!" and "Oh wow, what an asshole." "She is the supposed cousin of Aaron's that he was lying about." "She is actually the new booty...LMAO!"* I couldn't even be angry that he showed up with someone like that.

The twins kept going over to him, calling him Daddy and sitting on his lap and hugging him and kissing him, as they had no idea what was going on. At one point, he took them both out to the vending machine to get them a snack just before Jason's parents provided everyone with McDonalds. Myrtle is what I will call the "cousin." She kept looking at me like a question mark. It's like she was figuring out that something wasn't quite right with the picture. When she would look at me, I would give her a grin to let her know that her suspicion was correct.

My girls were sending me text messages of *"Mommy be good!" "Mommy, we are here for Jason, forget them, she's ugly and he's a piece of shit for bringing her here!"* They were right and I had to put myself in that mindset but it was hard with it being in my face. To me, she had no business at the hospital; she didn't even know Jason or Barbara. Then to make it even harder, Myrtle had apparently figured it all out. Realizing the situation, she looked over at me to catch my eye and then she leaned over toward King and they kissed. He actually kissed her back. (*At first I was pissed because if I tried to give him a peck on the cheek or show any type of affection, he would move away from me and say 'nooo, not in public, I know people,' and then he would look around and laugh as if he were making a joke, but I knew he was serious.*) After their moment, she looked back over to me and anger left my emotions and I had to laugh. I laughed in her face because she just didn't know our history. She was temporary and she was about to find out soon enough. When I laughed at her, the girls followed suit and she looked at all of us puzzled. That made us laugh even harder because of the look on her face through her glasses, they made her eyes look huge because she was wearing trifocals.

Jason's mother continued to give us updates of his condition and to let us know exactly when we could have our turn to go back and see him. Hours had gone by and Aaron, King and Myrtle went back before us. They must have spent at least 10 to 15 minutes or so before we went back. Passing them leaving, King kept his head down the entire time that he was in our presence and even more so when passing by me. We went into Jason's room and his appearance was hurtful. We didn't know what to say with him being in the condition that he was in. He was scraped up, patched up, stitched up, and wrapped up. I wanted to hold him and just squeeze him but couldn't so I gave him a long kiss on top of his head. Lisa began to cry. It was hard to see him this way. The twins kept asking, 'What's wrong with Uncle Jason?' We explained to them that he had been in a bad car accident and that was why they couldn't go back to see him but that they would be able to see him soon. We then headed back to our city.

The next day, I called King and we talked about how unbelievable everything was, how bad of a shape Jason was in, and the fact that Barbara was gone. We made plans to go to the funeral. We never once mentioned Myrtle as she was of no relevance to me and apparently of no relevance to him either. Later that night he kept texting me about wanting to make up. As usual, I went for it. We texted each other through the wee hours of the morning after I turned him down to spend the night with him. We talked about doing dinner nights again. We would always go out to dinner and each one of us would take turns paying. I think we had exhausted all the restaurants in our city. We always spent at least $50 to $80 each time because we had to have our drinks of Absolut, Heineken and a Long Island Iced Tea. It was nice because it was just us spending quality time and having great adult conversation. He later began to cook for me from various recipes. It was fun because he would call me to come over and help him and we would talk about our jobs, as he was finally opening up to me and talked about things that went on at his job, and I would talk to him and ask advice about my publishing company and authors and my foundation. I enjoyed this most about being with him because it was just him. It lasted for a good few months until it started to go back to the way it used to be with a houseful of mid 20's kids our children's ages as they cracked jokes on each other *(this always went too far)*, tried to out dance one another, play fighting and just get completely drunk and out of hand by showing off his guns. It went from mature nights to kiddie nights and then would get messy very quickly.

It didn't take long for King to start making mountains out of molehills again by picking a fight with me to push me away so he could go play. This one time in particular, he pushed me away so he and Aaron could go to McDuff's. He literally kicked me out of his house. I left with an expected argument but went to Frank's home where he was entertaining a new 'friend'. That was something Frank and I would do. He complained about his many women and I complained about King and we would give each other advice. His new 'friend' didn't seem to mind my being there so we all talked and discussed my problem…King. We stayed up and talked until 2AM and, just as I was headed home, I received a text from King stating that Myrtle had just left his house. I knew he was joking with me in order to get me to come over and I went. However, when I started to pull up, I spotted a white car pulling out of his driveway. It was Myrtle and Aaron's real cousin, Renee. I followed them down the street and they then circled around and shouted out at me.

"Is there a muthafuckin' problem?!"

"Your damn right there is…what are you doing at my boyfriend's house?!" I shouted back.

We pulled over to the side of the road and began to talk.

"Ooohhh, I knew it. She's the one from the hospital," Myrtle said to Renee while pointing over at me.

"Yes I am and he and I have been together going on two years now," I added.

"I knew it was something. He is a damn liar and so full of shit! I met him at McDuff's and knew him for a week and he told me about how his ex-wife left him with bills on top of bills and then said that his house was my house and to make myself comfortable, but he never mentioned you. Where were you for the week that I was there?" Myrtle asked

"He and I were on the outs for that week, but he was still texting me wanting us to get back together."

"I'm sorry and I understand. I just saw him tonight at McDuff's and he was following me around all night, wasn't he Renee?"

"Yup. I can't believe this. I thought he was cool and his place was gonna be a nice little hangout for us. Wow, that's fucked up!" said Renee.

At this point, King was calling me because he saw me follow them down the street and he was yelling for me to *get my ass back to his house.* Myrtle grabbed my phone and cussed him out calling him Napoleon syndrome and other bad words that actually hurt my feelings. She cussed him out pretty bad and then gave me back my phone.

"Ma, you will never have a problem out of me. I promise you that. I'm going home and going to bed because I got to get up early for work in the morning. I'm sorry." She said.

King continued to call my cell and when I didn't answer after talking with Myrtle and Renee, he began to text me, demanding that I get to his house ASAP.

"Look, there must be something there for him to keep calling you like this. I understand. Just go ahead cuz, it's obvious ya'll got love for each other," said Renee with an agreement from Myrtle. They both asked me to speak to them if I ever saw them out because they had no problem with me and hoped that I didn't have one with them. I assured them that we were okay and I drove off to King's house. As I pulled up in the driveway, King was coming down the walkway and then we saw Myrtle driving back down his street, this time Renee was in the passenger seat. Myrtle started yelling obscenities to King.

"Let's settle this once and for all...both of you come in the house," demanded King. "Look, I'm not with you and I'm not with you." I couldn't believe he said that but, then again, it was coming from him and I should have expected it, but it took me by surprise and pissed me off. Aaron started holding me back because I was going after his ass.

While Aaron was holding me back, he was explaining to me that King was just playing with me because he knew that if he told me that Myrtle was at the house, I would get jealous and come over, which is what he really wanted me to do. Aaron went onto say that he and King did go to McDuff's and saw Myrtle there but that King ignored her all night and when they got home, she pulled up and rung the doorbell and King went to the door and she asked him if she should stay or if she should go and he boldly and firmly told her to go and that was when I pulled up and saw them pulling out. Out of all the lies that everyone would say Aaron would tell and what a 'do boy' and co-signer he was, my spirit felt like he was telling me the truth. While Aaron was holding me back, King was kicking Myrtle out of his house. After he shut the door on her, I was about to leave and he forcefully yelled for me to *sit my ass down!'*

When we turned our back to go into the kitchen, we heard a loud crash. Myrtle had thrown a boulder through King's glass front door and sped off. King ran through the busted door and began to shoot his gun off into the air. He then came back through the busted door and said for us to call the cops. Aaron called and was talking to dispatch trying to explain what just took place but dispatch seemed to be more concerned with reports of gunshots. Aaron then handed me his phone to complete the call.

"No ma'am, there wasn't any gunshots." I then went onto explain what Myrtle did and dispatch ended the call with having the police come. I sat at the kitchen table watching King and Aaron clean up the glass and try to cover the door with a piece of plywood. The police came and asked questions of what happened exactly.

"This woman came to my house arguing with me and then with my girlfriend *(pointing to me. At times, I was his 'baby and girlfriend' when black men were around and I was just a friend when he was around other women or his white friends)* and when I told her to leave, she threw the boulder through my door," King lied.

We all then gave written statements against Myrtle. After I gave my statement and the police left, I told King that I was done with him and he said he was done with me and I told him that was his karma and that was what he gets for having someone he only knew for a week in his house, then I sped off. *(After court, Myrtle ended up having to pay King $300 in damages and received 6 months probation).* Our little argument only lasted for a few days. This was routine. Unhealthy routine, but it was us. It was also draining me in all aspects of emotions. My heart was hardening toward him and toward whatever this was we had going on. One thing for sure, I didn't love him like I used to. His past actions were fading my feelings toward him considerably. He was tarnished and tainted. It just wasn't the same.

Almost two weeks later Barbara's funeral came about. It was a closed casket with huge flowers on it and they had some of her favorite sports team's paraphernalia along with a flat screen TV that showed videos of her. It was touching and still unbelievable that she was actually gone. I sat at least four rows back from King as he was sitting with Jason and his mother and father. Afterwards, everyone began to socialize in the foyer of the funeral home where it was very overcrowded, so much so that I had to brush up against people just to get by. I was finally able to get outside and back to my truck. As I began to pull out of the parking lot, King called me and asked if I was okay. I relayed that I was okay and he told that he was heading home and wanted me to come by to get something to eat with him. Following routine, I did just that and followed him back to his house. We sat silently for awhile as we both tried to digest actually being at Barbara's funeral.

King finally broke the mutual silence and asked me if I signed the guest book and I informed him that I had. He then shared with me that "B's" mother had stood behind him and was looking over his shoulder in order to see what name he had signed and when she saw what he had signed his name as, she looked up at him and said, *'oh...your Damon', and* then she turned and walked away. At that moment, we were both puzzled as to why she wanted to know who King was, but we would soon find out.

15

❧

FOURTH OF JULY

Let no one deceive you with empty words, for because of these things the wrath of God comes upon the sons of disobedience.

EPHESIANS 5:6

Months had gone by and King and I were getting along beautiful-ly. *(I wanted to forget about the past and start my feelings over for him but something in my spirit was warning me to be careful and so I just enjoyed each good day and didn't look any deeper, just treasured my time with him moment by moment.)* We would talk or text each other during the day while working. I continued to take him lunch and, at times, cigarettes. He would text me when he got home and then he would call me and ask me to come over and we would do yard work together. If we didn't eat out, or if I brought him a plate, we would cook together from different recipes and eat dinner like we used to. I would clean up the kitchen while he folded the laundry. Later we would lock up the house and get to bed by 9:30/10PM, the latter after I would rub his shoulders down with ointment to relieve his pain from working so hard, and then we would cuddle until we fell asleep only to wake up at 5:30AM and do our routine over again that included taking a shower, watching the news, ironing work clothes, making breakfast, taking care of Spike and telling each other to have a good day with a parting hug and peck on the lips. Company was scarce and, on his days off, we would have overnight stays and watch a movie either at my house or his with the twins. It was nice to be in *'this place'* with him, but it didn't last long just like the past. Whenever we were in *'this place'* it was always disturbed. It never failed.

Company started coming around once again, stronger than ever, and he was showing his ass more than ever before as well. He was becoming more disrespectful and repeatedly talked about sleeping with other women. *(In his words, 'I would fuck her' talking about his supposedly friends' girlfriends, including Aaron's girlfriend and ex-girlfriends and women in random, it could be women on a TV show or commercial.)* The company would laugh and the more they laughed the more he put on a show for them. He started staying nights in the other cities again and did not contact me. He was getting more drunk than usual, to the point that he would pass out completely. It went from good to bad to worse to horrible after those several good months and I didn't know what had changed. The roller coaster ride was happening again. The routine was getting old but, for some reason, this incident was worse than ever before and I was finally fed up and enough was finally enough. *(Words often spoken, but never kept. I vowed to myself that if he mistreated me like the same ol' routine as before, I was walking for good.)*

The Fourth of July was a holiday meant for family and friends, but not for King. He didn't want me around. He had other plans. *(Every holiday, he would act like an asshole to me to push me away. His excuse was that he doesn't do holidays anymore since his ex-wife left him, therefore, he couldn't spend that time with me. It was all a crock of shit. It was on the fun holidays that he would make earlier plans that excluded me every time but included his friends, women and drinking.)* He came to my house for dinner after work a few days before the Fourth of July and we were doing okay. We had intentions of ordering a movie with the kids, eating dinner and just relaxing. After dinner was ready, I began making up some plates. He came into the kitchen.

"I know you didn't make my plate!" King unexpectedly stated.

"Yes. Why not?"

"You don't listen. That's all right. Your gonna learn yet. I can show you better than I can tell you," he threatened.

I didn't know what that threat meant and what the big deal was about making up his plate. Had he been referring to the day before when he and his friend, Lamont, had come to my house and I had fried fish for them and then made up their plates? He had made such a big thing out of me making his plate that he went home early and acted like he didn't want to talk to me anymore after I sent him a text asking what the big deal was. He was short with me and made it clear that he was done talking.

The next day I called him to see if we were still on for a social media event with the Chamber of Commerce because I had a badge made for him from a printing company with his company logo on it with his name underneath. Even though he said he wasn't going at that moment, I thought that maybe he would change his mind because this had been preplanned from the week before. He stated, however, that he wasn't going because he was mad at me for accusing him of cheating. I never accused him of cheating. *The day after he left my house, mad because I made his dinner plate, I called him later that evening at around 8:30PM and he answered with an attitude like he didn't want to talk to me and his words were very short. I asked him what was he doing and he sounded muffled. I asked again because I didn't hear him very well as his cell phone was cutting out and he then yelled at me that he was asleep. I said okay and he hung up abruptly. If I ever called him while he was sleeping, he would answer and just tell me calmly that he was asleep and say that he would call back when he got up. But this time he didn't do this. He was still upset with me.*

When Aaron had a party at the house, I heard about it via Aaron's media page and I told King that with a party going on, I knew he wasn't asleep the entire time he stated to me. He said that he was until around 3AM when he got up and went downstairs and spoke to everyone and drank a beer, had a shot of vodka with them and went back to bed. Not once did I suggest to him that he was cheating on me. Those words never came out of my mouth, but he heard what he wanted to hear and told everybody those were my words.

Fourth of July morning and we were still not speaking. Not surprised at all. He didn't text and if I texted him, he wouldn't reply or respond to my calls. He completely ignored me. I then received a text from Karen, a wanna be black, amazon, white girl that was an ex to Jason. *(Yes King had her number too like I mentioned earlier that he would stay in contact with his friends ex's to come chill with him after their breakup either at his house or he would go to theirs and stay nights.) Karen was a busy body that invented drama and always thought of herself as a gift to black men, as she would put it, 'They all asked about the white girl with the black girl booty.' She mistook her extremely widespread, 250 pound, 6' foot 2" ass as a donkey. She didn't know it, but within our circle, they always talked about her behind her back and she was known as a ho, especially when she gave one of the guys a blow job in King's house on his couch and King actually allowed it. She was a snake too and would throw you under the bus if she had the opportunity. She was the type that if you were doing well, she was doing better and if you had something that was nice, she used to have that or she had something better.* She text me and asked if I was coming to King's house to celebrate the Fourth. For some reason, I felt like she already knew we were bugging, but I guess she wanted my take on it, so I did what King always said, *'throw a dog a bone'* and that's what I did. I told her that we were not speaking and explained the whole made his plate bullshit and she pretended to be surprised and said for me to show up anyway. I told her that I'd rather not but that I was going to bug the shit out of him and make like I was going to pop up to make him nervous. She then stated that she would help me out and give me a play by play of what was going on at his house and would let me know if he brought any chicks there. Of course I went along with her doing that because I didn't think she would actually do it. I had always known her to be full of shit. So I thought she was lying to me, but she surprised me.

I received a text from her telling me that from my many text messages to King about me coming over there, he was getting paranoid and started worrying that I was going to make good on my threats of showing up. A few hours later, she stated that his friend Lamont showed up with two ugly crack head looking black girls and King asked Lamont *'which one is for me?'* At that moment, I was more than pissed. I really wanted to come over for real then, but I didn't. I waited. I waited to get back at him with his Cadillac. *Several months back, King put his Cadillac in my name for when he was ready to file bankruptcy, it wouldn't show that he had too many assets and then after the bankruptcy, I would sign it back over to him. I was down for all that, no problem, but I was fed up with his disrespect and disregard of my feelings and I wanted revenge. Yes it was wrong, but I had nothing else because I didn't cheat.* I began texting him back to back and calling him and he wouldn't respond to either one. I then called the nonemergency number to the police station and asked them to meet me at his house because I wanted *'my'* car back from my ex-boyfriend's house, which was a lie I was willing to tell the police. I told them that he gave it to me as a gift, *for which later King sent me a text that I still have til this day stating that he doesn't want to take the car out of my name and that it's my car.* I told the police that he wanted to change the oil in it and after he did, I had too much to drink at his house and he took me home but wouldn't give the car back. They checked on the registration and stated that it was absolutely my car and they escorted me to his house to retrieve it.

Later that night, King pretended not to be home and wouldn't answer the police officer's knock on the door or doorbell ring. Since there was nothing that could be done because there was no response from King, they asked me if I knew of any of his friends' numbers so they could relay a message to him. Karen informed me that King, Lamont and the two crack heads all went to watch the fireworks together and later went to McDuff's, so I had them call Lamont's cell. Lamont stated that he and the two crack heads were back in there nearest city and dropped King off, but I didn't believe him. Since that was a no go for the police, they told me to try again the following day.

Shortly after my departure from the police and King's house, I received a text from Lamont calling me all kinds of bitches and skanks and said my mother was a ho and that I was a muthafucker and that I needed to get some dick...just all kinds of obscenities, then he sent another text saying, "it's not your car bitch, fuck you ho, never call me again!" He kept sending these messages back to back, nonstop, for an hour and I still didn't hear from King.

The next day I was still heated from all the information Karen had given me, to King not answering my calls or text, and to Lamont sending me those nasty messages. I wanted revenge and I wanted it now more than ever so I once again called the police and had an officer escort me back to King's house. Karen's car was in the driveway. She then sent me a long ass text message saying that I was going about the whole thing wrong and that she is still going to hang out with King regardless and that I was wrong about the entire situation and that she shouldn't have to choose between him and me. That 'choosing' part threw me off because I never asked her to choose between us, that was so childish and she was the one that decided she wanted to give me a play by play of what was going on in his house. She was really trippin' on me. I couldn't believe it. Our so called friendship was over between us as far as I was concerned. I was done with her.

This wasn't the first time Karen had tried to play me. At one point before this particular incident, King and I were on the outs for a few days and she was all in the mix as usual. She is known as a 'ho', 'drama queen' and 'busy body'. The two young brothers *(of course she was screwing the older brother but you would think she was with the younger one from the too close interaction between them of constantly and secretly texting one another while the other brother was sitting in the very same room and they were always going off alone together. Having too much to drink one night, she asked me my opinion about her sleeping with the younger brother. I told her to leave him where he is and only deal with the older brother before the situation turned ugly.)* Karen, her girlfriend, and King all went to another city to have dinner and enjoy a place that played Reggae live. Being that King and I later became friends, she purposely placed pictures on his wall to spite me *(per King after he and I made up)*. She posted pictures of them having a ball the entire weekend he and I were not speaking. Him hugging another woman smiling, him at McDuff's with the brothers and our circle. She was being a bitch to me and she and I were not even on bad terms, or so I thought.

Seeing the pictures on his wall really hurt me deeply. It was like he didn't care at all about me and he had simply allowed someone else to hurt me as well. He had control over the situation but he used her in order to make me jealous. For the most part of that weekend, he continued to ignore my calls and text messages. When he finally did answer, he told me that he wanted to hangout with other people and he didn't want me with him. *I felt that he could have told me that in a better way instead of showing me in the manner he had done so. In the past when things were going awry with him acting as if he were single, pushing me away and starting no nonsense arguments, he would say or do things, leaving it open with regards to being with another woman, so I would ask him and he would reply with 'whatever, think what you want to think, I'm tired of you accusing me of things'...and that would be his way out. The* one time he did answer, I couldn't hold the tears back any longer and I boo hoo cried my eyes out to him, asking him to stop treating me this way and to please talk to me. Needless to say, he blew me off so harshly with 'I will talk to you later', hung up and never answered my calls or text again for the rest of the weekend.

Within a matter of a week or so, I stopped calling and texting him and put my head into my career, which was going quite well. I was beginning to get King out of my system and I was feeling good about it. I felt like a burden had been lifted and I didn't have any stress. I no longer had to deal with his drama. It felt good to be around my female colleagues and not have to be embarrassed with King making passes at them, with foul sexual remarks and trying to entice them with talks about how he has a big pool house and can cook and would cook for them and that he had money buried in his backyard and would bury money for them too when he changed their last name to his. I would be more than embarrassed. They would laugh along, but I later heard snide remarks that were said behind my back in regards to King and his drunken words and, as for my male colleagues, they wondered what I was doing with him. They always told me that I needed to deal with men of better caliber because King was beneath me. Needless to say, the communication amongst my colleagues and I began to fade. As for some of them, we don't speak at all anymore and, as for others, it's more fake than anything else and, as for the real colleagues, we talk all the time.

My mind was relaxed and my thoughts were healthy along with my emotions, but you know how it goes, when all is good, the enemy will show up. King started calling me, but I wouldn't answer. Then he would send text messages and I wouldn't respond. His next move would always be to call my house or text Arielle to try to get her to talk me into communicating with him. He was a snake and when he felt like he wasn't getting anywhere with my daughter because I still wouldn't get in touch with him, he would show up at my doorstep, ringing my bell and banging on my door talking through it as if he were holding a conversation with me. I did not understand him at all. He would push me away because he didn't wish for me to be in his presence, lie to people telling them that I had a really bad attitude, told other's 'fuck me' and that he didn't want to be with me anymore and even went as far as to say that I would beg him to come back to me. People believed him I guess but it didn't matter to me what they believed because I have always known that the truth would come to light so I would give up and grant him his wish and when he realized that, he would try everything to be in my presence. Therefore, the lies that he told were revealed and made him look like an ass because he was the one begging. He would try to justify his ways by saying to me *you know how I am by now* as if it was to excuse his ignorance and disrespect and chalk it up like it's okay because that was just him...I felt like I was finally fed up. A few days later, Damon sent me a text to ask where I was. I told him I was on the trails jogging, so he came to me with this letter.

7-9-12   8:20 PM   MON.

I WANT TO START THIS LETTER OUT BY SAYING I CANT DO THIS! I CARE ABOUT YOU AND DONT WANT TO LOOSE YOU LIKE THIS. I AM REALLY LONELY WITHOUT YOU AND IT IS JUST NOT RIGHT WITHOUT YOU HERE.

WE WILL ALWAYS HAVE ARGUEMENTS BUT IT DOESNT HAVE TO TAKE THIS LONG TO MAKE UP.

IN A RELATIONSHIP, ITS HOW FAST YOU BOUNCE BACK, NOT HOW LONG YOU STAY MAD AT EACH OTHER.

I NEED YOU AND I HOPE THAT YOU NEED ME TO. I TOLD YOU BEFORE THAT IT WASANT GOING TO BE PEACHES + CREAM. GO BACK TO THE COMMUNICATION THING WHEN WE ARE SOBER AND NOT MAD. THINGS ARE SAID AND DONE OUT OF ANGER, NOT WHAT WE REALLY ~~FEE~~ FEEL.

STOP THE MADNESS AND COME BACK HOME. IT IS TOO EMPTY HERE WITHOUT YOU.

CANT EAT, CANT SLEEP, CANT THINK STRAIGHT WITHOUT YOU.

YOU FIGHT FOR WHAT YOU WANT AND IM WILLING TO GO AS MANY ROUNDS AS I HAVE TO.

This was the Damon that I knew. This was my King. This is how he was toward me when we were alone without the negative influences and that was what kept me going back to him even after his mistreatment because I felt like I knew the inner him. The real him that no one else knew. This was a man that would run my bath water, light candles, and bathe me after I had a long hard workout, wash my hair, blow dry it, grease my scalp and even flat iron my hair for me. He pampered me his way. We would lie next to each other in bed at night and hold hands until we drifted off to sleep after having long conversations about nothing. No one could understand why I was in love with Damon because they saw how he talked to me in front of them when that liquor was in his system and they saw how he treated me with disrespect by sleeping with other women because they were hanging out with him, but he was wonderful to me whenever we were alone. The letter touched my heart and I felt like he really meant those words. I must have read that letter at least 10 times, going to sleep and waking up with it in my hands, praying that his words were sincere and true. I needed for those words to be just that.

16

So Tired!

Come to me, all who labor and are heavy laden, and I will give you rest. Take my yoke upon you, and learn from me, for I am gentle and lowly in heart, and you will find rest for your souls. For my yoke is easy, and my burden is light.

Matthew 11:28–30

We began cooking at each other's houses again and fell back into our 'good' routine of great communication, going to football games and Chamber of Commerce events together, which was always fun because we would see how many people we would know and he always won with knowing way more because of the line of work he was in. It was like he knew everyone there and for the ones he didn't know, they got to know him real quick and he wasn't even a member.

We made our own fun everywhere we went and would just enjoy one another. Company at his house was not so heavy or maybe just a few from our circle would come once in awhile and, for the most part, it was just King and I joking, laughing and loving on each other. It was beautiful and I felt like we were getting closer. He even began to open up to me about everything, especially of his days at work. We played around with each other and would have farting contests, but it was more like he was in the contest all by himself because he could fart on demand whereas I would let out the silent but deadly randomly.

We both loved the cherry licorice and we would steal them from each other. I always made fun of the way King would say it *(lik-whish) as* he could never say it correctly no matter how hard he tried. There was no more grumpiness in the morning, in fact, he would squeeze me tight, tell me he loved me and give me continuous kisses all over my face, telling me "thank you" continuously, and would say how he wished we could just stay in bed this way all day. Mornings and days like this were occurring on a daily basis and I was enjoying every minute of it. I felt like we were finally where we needed to be in our relationship. We were growing closer together. He would tell me he loved me more often and he wasn't even drunk when saying it. I was in awe! He began telling his friends that would try to urge him to go out that he wasn't going anywhere without 'his Baby'. I'm sure they probably didn't like that but I didn't care. I loved it and they had to respect it.

We were going strong for at least 3-4 months straight and our time spent together eased us into a few months shy of two years of courtship. He was being good to me, he was respectful, and treated me like I actually meant something to him and he didn't care if his friends knew it or if he showed it. For the first time in months, and I do mean months, I could feel his love for me and my feelings for him began to once again grow strong as all of the ill feelings I had developed for him in the past were fading away. I thought that he had finally gotten it, like he had fully matured and alcohol no longer played a major role because he wasn't drinking as much. He was in his right mind until another holiday came up…Labor Day.

Two days before Labor Day he was displaying distance toward me, but at the same time he was being extra nice. He always told me that if he was ever extra nice, I needed to worry because that meant he was up to something or if he never answered the phone for me, that meant he was with another woman. He even started back drinking heavier and would spend down to the penny to secure his vodka, beer and cigarettes. From his display and remembering the words spoken, it led me to believe that he had made plans and his plans did not include me. Sad to say, I was right. He pretended he had plans with Lamont, but judging from the many text messages and phone calls he was receiving from the ho's Jason used to sleep with all wee hours of the night and morning that would wake me up, he obviously had plans with whomever was communicating with him. His theory was he didn't want to spend holidays with someone he cared about, so he would rather spend it elsewhere with other people. He also stated that he could do whatever he wanted to do because I was not his wife. I reminded him that I was his girlfriend, but that held no weight. That was a crock of bullshit and I was more than tired of his ignorance and blatant disrespect.

"What about the other holidays coming up like Halloween, Thanksgiving, Christmas, New Year's Eve and Valentine's Day? Are you not going to spend any of those holidays with me either?" I screamed.

"I don't know. You know how I am by now; just let me get through this my way," he argued.

"This is such bullshit and it has gotten old real fast! It has been almost three years that she left you and your divorce is final and you're still acting like holidays are a problem, but you're quick to spend it with other women or other people in general. I'm done. She doesn't give a damn about the holidays because she's spending it with her man. I can't take this shit no more! I free you of me because the last thing I want is to be a burden on someone!" I cried.

"Just stop okay! Go! Get out!" he demanded with his finger pointing toward the door.

Aaron looked at me and asked where was I going and just when he asked, King nudged him to be quiet. As I was walking out, King followed me with a look in his eyes as if he knew he went too far this time. The look was as if he was sorry but he was still going to do what he was going to do. To me, that meant he didn't care and he didn't give a damn about me. I was more than hurt. I was livid and my first instinct was to hurt him in all aspects of physical, mental and emotional abuse. I wanted to hurt him bad physically for wasting almost two years of my life. I wanted so badly for him to feel the pain that I was feeling so he could see how horrible it felt so he would stop hurting me. Hate began to boil in my blood toward him because he made me feel like the love I gave him and how good I treated him meant nothing at all. He even had the nerve to say that he knows I'm good to him so my question is why treat me like shit then?! I couldn't take it anymore. My career and companies were doing very well and I was in the public eye in a great and positive way and I couldn't allow his mistreatment toward me affect my emotions. I told him *'I free you of me'* and I meant that from the bottom of my heart even now regardless if we ever talk again.

It hurt like hell to say that to him because I wanted nothing more than to be with this man, but I knew nothing would change. It would have been the same cycle of things being good for a few months followed by things turning bad, then going back to being good for another few months before things then got even worse. It was all too much to bear. Blatant disrespect and no regard for my feelings were appalling to me. He said that we were not in a relationship, but his actions showed different and we lived like we were in a committed relationship until whenever he decided to think with that wrong head and then he would give me his ass to kiss until he was done playing. Afterwards, I would get words much like the words from his letter to me and the bad cycle would start all over again. Enough was finally enough. I even went as far as to change my cell phone number. My home number, I couldn't change because it was tied to my foundation for three years.

It was time to let him go and walk away for good. No contact, no remorse, no hate, no regrets of ever meeting him. I had to pray and ask God to remove the hate, remorse and regrets from my heart and mind, as well as the dreadful emotional attachment I had with him. It was time to let go of all of him in all aspects from every angle. I had to move on and accept moving on without him in my life. I couldn't be his friend because he was poison to me. Just no good at all and if I allowed myself to continue on his venomous ride, then all that I have worked so hard for would have diminished slowly but surely. All the drinking that he does for sure would have destroyed me because I followed behind him. As far as the twins not seeing or hearing from 'Daddy', I never said anything at all.

I was sitting on my bed just staring blankly with tears in my eyes and thinking about the decision I made in regards to King when Arielle walked into my room to have a talk with me about the situation and to try and give me some good advice.

"Mommy, it seems like drinking, partying and lusting are Damon's priorities. God has so much waiting for you. You can't let anyone deter you from your destiny. Just stay in prayer and I will pray for you and for Damon."

She then gave me a book called "Every Day I Pray" by Iyanla Vanzant that was filled with prayers for every life situation along with a scripture from the Bible:

'Ecclesiastes 4:13-16 – It is better to be a poor but wise youth than an old and foolish king who refuses all advice. Such a youth could rise from poverty and succeed. He might even become king though he has been in prison but then everyone rushes to the side of yet another youth who replaces him. Endless crowds stand around him but then another generation grows up and rejects him too. So it is all meaningless – like chasing the wind.' (Per Arielle, this means all of his so called friends are only around him for but a moment, but once the well runs dry and the party is over, they will rush to another source. So he may have the limelight temporarily because he likes being the center of attention, but real soon, it's all going to come to an end. He's going to end up alone and still angry and bitter.)

"See Mommy, Damon used different outlets to cope with his ex-wife leaving and divorcing him. I believe he stopped believing in God after that happened and that's where the alcoholism and other bad habits and lusting after people came into play stronger than ever and he idolizes those things. I believe that is why he jokes about God so much in a negative way because he has no faith in Him anymore. He knows of God and he knows what God can do for him, but he chooses to go the wrong path because he's still angry and that's why he keeps all the young kids around him to keep from being alone with his thoughts. Damon knows that the things he has done and is doing is wrong and he knows that he could have treated you better just let God deal with him."

Arielle's spoken words touched me in a way that made me not only think hard, but think clear. She was correct in every word she spoke to me and God was using her to close this door that needed to be shut almost two years ago when I noticed this behavior from Damon. I realize now that I allowed myself to be sucked in and God used many incidents to pull me back and when I was dismissing what was being brought to my attention, the situation got worse. I sat and listened and allowed Arielle's words to embed in my spirit and I moved on along my journey that God had placed before me of a successful nonprofit organization and publishing company.

17

⚘

LETTING GO

*For I know the plans I have for you, declares the Lord, plans for welfare and
not for evil, to give you a future and a hope.*

JEREMIAH 29:11

hree weeks had gone by without Damon and I speaking and I was
in a good place by way of my emotions, mentally, physically and
career-wise until I heard a rumor that he was seeing a much older
woman that was lacking tremendously in the 'looks' department that re-
sided in another city. *(He always went for the ghetto-type females in looks,
speech and demeanor, no matter the age or color, and they would have nothing going for themselves. He just went for anything and this was carried out
randomly, as well as constantly with an 'I don't care' attitude. He always said
he can do what he wanted whenever he wanted and he was never gonna
stop being who he is. 'I will always be me' per him, but the kicker was that he
never strapped up (he didn't with me) and that bothered me, which was why
I stopped having relations with him. He was careless with his whole being
and just slept with anyone and everyone that would let him whether it was
with his friend's girlfriends, wives, baby's mama's or ex-girlfriends. That type
of behavior took any respect I had for him away completely and I saw him
in a different light. He even stooped so low as to have his son text me a lie
after he would not answer the phone for me, stating that he was at his son's*

apartment, asleep, when he was really at a hotel room with one of his friend's kid's mother who just got out of rehab for drugs, crack in particular, which led her to have a crack baby. She ran off at the mouth with telling mutual friends about her and him being together and according to her, it wasn't the first time. I was more than disappointed in him. He wasn't a 'King' he was just Damon, a typical, immature, dirty old man that was an angry, bitter alcoholic with a one track mind. It puzzled me as to why he was the way he was because he came from good breed. I spent time with his parents, a beautiful couple that I adore...I just didn't get it.)

On my way home from working out with my trainer, I spotted Damon across the street from me at a red light with this mystery woman on the passenger side of his truck. He didn't notice me because I had bought a new car shortly after we broke up. This woman's thick glasses and very obvious old lady hair wig made me stare her down even more to scope out the rest of her and the rumors were right, she was not a looker at all, dark as night, and it made me wonder what he was doing with her, as she did not look to even be a 'clean' person or even his type. After I got home, out of jealousy again, I found software via the Internet to text Damon so he wouldn't get my new cell number and I was being mean.

"WOW what the hell are you doing with that ugly ass woman?! She looks like shit, old and dirty and makes you look the same. You just couldn't stand being alone huh? I can't even get jealous, but glad she makes you happy."

"I tried to talk to you, but you wouldn't answer, and I texted you and you wouldn't return my text messages." He text back.

"I changed my cell number; so I did not receive any of your messages," I texted.

"I love you always and forever and I owe you everything!" he replied.

"I love you always and forever too and you owe me nothing, as everything and anything I ever did for you was from my heart." I returned.

"Everything that I will do for you will be from my heart as well," he responded.

We must have texted back and forth for at least two hours straight. I felt much better to have communicated with him and I could tell he felt the same. I know I was falling back into the trap, but for some reason, this time; it was different regardless if that woman was there. She was so gone that you couldn't even consider her temporary. The next day Damon called the house phone and told Arielle that he was coming by to pick up the twins after he got off work. I had an installation dinner with one of the organizations I was a member of at the time he got off so I did not see him at all that night but heard about what a wonderful time the twins had with 'Daddy'. He took them out to eat and shot pool and shuffle board with them at McDuff's, which was kid friendly during dinnertime.

Still not giving up my new cell number, I texted Damon again via Internet and thanked him.

"They will always be my children," he replied.

Damon then called the house and asked me to come by so he could show me the other plans he had set for them. I went over and we ate Chinese food together and he was dead ass serious about his plans with the twins, as he had printed directions to their destinations and one of them was a petting zoo. Once we finished eating and chatted about the twins, I thanked him again and we hugged and he walked me out to my car. I remember thinking on my way home how nice that was, but I knew that it was all part of his plan and sooner or later something would happen to tarnish it and we would be back to not speaking again. The next day, I called Damon at work and asked him about this woman. He was open to communication in her regard and I asked him questions like a high school girl with a huge crush.

"Where did you meet her?" I inquired.

"I met her at Lamont's cousin's cookout in Oberlin," he replied.

"Do you have feelings for her? I mean do you really like her?" I asked.

"No I don't have feelings for her and no I don't really like her," he responded.

"Then why are you with her?" I asked.

"It was just something to do and she is not my girlfriend," he answered.

"What's her name?" I asked.

"I'm not telling you her name. What's your new cell number?" he laughed.

"You don't get to have that yet," I said.

"Well fuck you then nigga! Bye!" he laughed.

We both started laughing. He was always so silly and always knew how to make me laugh and turn something serious into a chuckle.

"Well I just wanted to say hypothetically that if we were to get back together that I need you to treat me better. I need respect and someone that is going to be in my corner not halfway, but all the way and treat me just as good as I treat you. If I give 100% then you give me the same if not more. I need a man, Damon, and I want someone in my life, as well as the twins' lives; no half steppin' and I want you to be the man I need you to be. Be by my side, stay in my corner and give me what I will give you and you know I will give 110% of myself and I expect that from you. Be my ride or die because you know I will be that for you. It's time to grow up." I demanded.

"I know. I know and if we were to get back together, I will be all those things. Let's just take it one day at a time," he responded.

"If we got back together, will you continue communication with this woman?" I asked.

"No I will not. I have to go, but I will call you when I get off work," he said.

Damon called the house as promised and asked Arielle to tell me to call him because I still refused to give him my new cell number. I was at the grocery store when Arielle called me to relay Damon's message. I called Damon after checking out, but called him blocked. He asked me what I wanted to eat because he was starving. I told him I was undecided and he suggested I come by his house to pick him up so we could go to one of our favorite restaurants. I dropped the groceries off at home and informed Arielle that Damon and I were going out to dinner. She chuckled with a smirk on her face, shaking her head side to side that I ignored. After picking Damon up, we arrived at the restaurant and we had our usual of turkey minis, fries with mine, and a baked potato for Damon served with a salad for both of us and a shot of Absolut, Heineken and a Long Island Iced Tea. As normal, Damon would mix my Long Island up just how I liked it and give it a taste test for me. We sat across from each in silence, just staring at one another with admiration and a smile.

"I missed you Baby," Damon uttered.

"I missed you too," I said.

"Now what were we talking about earlier about us getting back together?" he asked.

"I was just saying hypothetically speaking and I wanted you to know how I felt as far as my demands," I replied.

"I understand what you're saying and your right. Now I'm going to be honest with you. I love you. I love you so much Baby, but the fist fighting was too much for me," he said.

"You would start with me on purpose and say awful remarks to me and call me out with names and you think that I wouldn't want to punch you in the mouth?!" I interrupted.

"I know. I did start it because I know how to push your buttons and you let me. I don't want you to let me push your buttons and I know my mouth is really bad, but you can't fight me because you're not going to win. I don't like putting my hands on you and I'm so sorry for doing it for the times that I did. I was totally wrong for that. You know I would think to myself, why would she still come back to me knowing that I did that to her and I knew then that it was because you loved me. You truly loved me and I see it. I know you do Baby and I know that we are supposed to be together. As for the holiday thing, I feel like holidays should be spent with family, not that you and the babies aren't my family, but..."

"You mean you and your ex-wife and the boys?" I interrupted.

"Yes. I know I have to move on, but it's hard to do that right now because I am madly in love with my ex-wife, but I know that she and I would never work because I no longer trust her and I know she would leave me again and then I have you. You were going to be my next wife. I am in love with you Baby. I am, but I don't want to hurt you anymore because I'm not right. I know I'm not. I have to get myself together before I start a relationship, but I don't want to lose you and I would be a fool to let you go. Nobody is going to take care of me like you do. I know it's not fair to you, but I will always be in your life and those children's lives. You are not going to get rid of me. I just want you to be happy and if that means you being happy with someone else, then be with someone else, but I'm not going anywhere," he explained.

"So what are you saying, for me to find someone else?" I asked.

"Yes Baby, find someone else," he said looking away from me with glassy eyes.

I started to cry and he asked that I stop because his teary eyes were beginning to form like tears.

"Baby, I don't want to keep making you pay for what happened to me. I have been screwed by other people so bad that my motto now is to screw others before they screw me. I don't want to keep taking it out on you when it's not you I'm mad at," he confessed.

"But that's making you bitter," I said.

"Yes it is. I am bitter, but I love you so much and I don't want to keep hurting you. I know you love me and I love being with you. When we were together, you made me forget about everything and I mean everything, including my ex-wife. You're the only woman after her that I allowed to get that close to me and it scares me. I let you get too close and that is why I would push your buttons to push you away. I am being completely honest with you Baby, not to hurt your feelings but to let you know that I truly love you and I love the way you love me. Nobody took care of me the way you have and nobody ever will. You always got my back. You and Robbie are the only one's that ever looked out for me. I will do anything for you and you can have whatever you want from me. I mean it. You need anything, you got it. I owe you for so much, Baby. Whatever you want it's yours. I'm gonna take care of you. I love you so mu....excuse me," he said.

Damon then excused himself up from the table and headed into the restroom, as he was tearing up. When Damon returned we continued our conversation.

"I wanted us to take this time away from each other to reflect on what we needed to do internally to make a change for the better so we could be better for each other but, instead, you continued to run in circles and let strangers in," I said.

"And you're right. I opened myself up to everybody to keep from getting hurt," he replied.

"But you're only hurting yourself by doing that. Do you understand that?" I asked.

"Yes I understand and I will change. Right now, let's do whatever it is that you want to do," he suggested, getting off the subject.

"I don't know. I'm not hard to please, I'm pretty easy going," I smiled.

"Ahhh, there it is...you have a beautiful smile Baby and those eyes and that nose ring, mmmm, mmmm, but your head is still bigger than a muthafucker tho, you big headed fucker!" he joked. We laughed so hard. We then decided to go back to my house where Damon stayed the night with the twins. He played with them way past their bedtime, then finally put them to bed and came into my bedroom where he made a bed for himself on the floor with my blanket and several throw pillows I make my bed up with. We watched TV until the TV was watching us. The next morning, he got up with the twins and took them to their bus stop with hugs and kisses of seeing 'Daddy' later. I then took Damon home to get a change of clothes and since it was his day off, he and I went back to my house. We spent the day together watching a movie, making dinner and had more conversation of hypothetically getting back together.

"What is it that you want Baby...tell me?" he asked.

"If we get back together Damon, I want the woman gone, I want a ring on my finger and I want the twins and me to live with you in your house so I can finish decorating where I left off," I answered.

"I have no problem with that Baby. What do you want, 3 karats or 5 karats?" he asked.

"Just something simple," I replied.

"No Baby, I will get you something special and as for the house, Robbie will keep his room for when he comes to visit and the babies will have the back room to share and we need to finish cleaning it out too," he suggested.

It was about that time for the twins' bus to arrive at their stop and Damon went and picked them up. After dinner, Damon suggested that he and I go to the beach for a walk and more conversation. We did just that and it was refreshing. I enjoyed being with him and my heart and mind were relaxed. Even though Damon and I did not establish ourselves as being a 'couple' we still spent quality time together and he kept his vow of being a father to the twins for the time being, as long as we stayed in communication with picking them up, taking them to his house to spend time with them and taking them out to eat or he would come to our house and spend time with them and make us dinner. He was staying nights as well and still slept on the floor beside my bed with a blanket and pillow. I could see that he was trying with putting forth effort.

A few days went by and I received a phone call from one of my colleagues, Carl, that lived in Oberlin. He had no idea that Damon and I had broken up.

"Hey Carl," I answered.

"Hey you, what's going on?" Carl asked with an inquisitive tone.

"What do you mean?" I asked.

"I heard that Damon was fucking around with Mabel Teasley. What the fuck is that about? If that's true, tell him for me that he needs to think that over because she is all about money. She going around talking about this new nigga she just hooked up with that had a big house with a pool and two cars and how he spends his money on her and what not and how he let her stay in his crib and shit while he be working and they do shit together on the weekends. I mean, she's talking like she got it like that, like it's her shit already. I didn't even know who this broad was talking about until she described ol' boy and then I knew when she said a short dude with gold teeth. I put two and two together with the house and pool and shit and I remembered from when you first told me you two were going out and the pictures you had up on your media page and that's what made me call you to see what was up," Carl explained.

"Yeah, he and I broke up and instead of taking that two weeks to internalize, he went for anything," I said.

"Yeah, Baby girl, you got that right because Mabel ain't shit. Tell that brother to run and run fast. She's nothing but a drunk, a snoop and a user. She a broke, ghetto ass, old head. Look here, tell that nigga I said to open his fuckin' eyes and see what the fuck he got in front of him before I take you! That bitch ain't no fuckin' good, and you know I know, that I know, that I know," Carl devilishly laughed.

"Yeah I know nasty boy and you couldn't have me!" I laughed.

"She will take him for everything he's got, she's a broke ho. She tried me and went through my personal shit that's why I got what the fuck I wanted and left that old ass broad alone!" Carl said.

"Wow bro', really? Damn. I'm gonna call him right now. He at work," I said.

"Alright Baby girl. Be careful and hit me up sometime," Carl added.

I called Damon immediately and he was his happy normal self, joking with me. I started off stuttering, not knowing quite what to say or how to say it.

"Are you busy?" I asked.

"A little, why nigga, what you want?" he joked.

"Do you still call and text that woman?"

"Yes, and she still calls and texts me," he said.

"Look, I don't know what you told that woman, but apparently you gave her confidence because she is going around talking shit," I said.

"Wh...What are you talking about?" he asked.

"Well, I know someone that knows Mabel Teasley and I mean knows her, knows her and she is not a good person and not who you think she is. She's going around talking about you're her boyfriend and what ya'll do and gonna do this weekend. I mean, Damon, you don't even know her and you let her all up and through your house and you only knew her for a few weeks. You can't trust everybody Damon. She is only after what she thinks you have. You're opening yourself up to strangers. You take her to your house and showoff the cars. She thinks you've got money and she is gonna want you to take care of her. Stop letting strangers in your house Damon. You act like I'm so damn awful, but this woman is gonna really stick it to you and you're gonna see what awful really is and then you will realize just how good I was to you. I never asked you for a penny Damon, ever! I would never do that to you. I don't give a damn if you have money or don't have money! And if you're still with her, she is never to be around those twins! Do you hear me?" I yelled.

"Yes and I would not do that," Damon answered quietly.

"I love you and I gotta get in the shower because I just got back from my workout and I have to go pay rent. I will talk to you later," I said.

"Okay," Damon said with a low voice sounding sad.

Twenty minutes later Damon called the house and Arielle informed him that I was in the shower and he requested that I call him back. After I got myself together, I gave Damon a call.

"Hey, you called?" I said.

"Did you wash stinky?" Damon joked.

"Yes farty!" I laughed.

"Well, someone came by my job today and gave me a gift," Damon explained.

"Really? What?" I inquired.

"Two football tickets to the Jaguars, end zone, November 25th," he said.

"Ooohhh yay! We can get a hotel room and everything and I will drive and...." I paused and we both laughed.

"Wait a minute; you didn't say I could go," I laughed.

"No I didn't nigga, but would you like to go?" he asked laughing.

"YES! Ooohh yay! Thank you!" I said.

"Your welcome and you probably will get mad at me before time, but you better be good and not call me with anymore shit," he joked.

"I was just looking out for my Babies' Daddy," I laughed.

"I know you were and I appreciate it. Thank you and I will talk to you later because I have to get back to work," he said.

"Okay, bye." We hung up.

Hours later, the twins came up to me and asked, "Mommy is Daddy still coming over cuz he said he was?" asked baby girl.

"I don't think so sweetie," I said.

"But he did say it cuz he was gonna help us bury our dead birdie," my baby boy announced.

"Give Daddy a call and ask him then because I don't know babies," I said.

Baby girl called Damon and asked him if he was coming over and he told her that he wasn't home, but in the next city with uncle Lamont. He then requested that she hand me the phone.

"Hey Baby, did I promise the twins I was coming over?" he asked.

"That's what they were telling me, but I didn't expect you today," I said.

"I probably did, but Baby, I'm with Lamont and his cousin. I will be home no later than 10PM because I have to go to work in the morning. Just tell my babies that I will see them tomorrow, but I won't be coming over tonight okay?" Damon said.

"Okay, I will," I said.

"Okay Baby, I will call you when I'm on my way home," he said.

"Okay," I said smiling.

I explained to the twins that Daddy would see them tomorrow. It was a long day and I still wasn't finished with work completely. I had to tie up loose ends with my publishing company and check out my scheduled meetings for the following week. As I completed my tasks, I called Damon because it was getting late.

"Hey, are you okay?" I asked.

"Hey Baby, yes, I'm okay. Me and Lamont are going to a strip club," he laughed.

"Are you really?" I laughed.

"Yes Baby, we are...really."

"Okay silly. Did you eat?" I asked.

"Yes. We are about to eat some oysters and I'm about to fuck the oysters up," he replied.

"Okay, just call me later," I laughed.

An hour and a half later, Damon called and told me that he left Lamont at the strip club because 10PM was quickly approaching and he wanted to get home to bed before it got too late. He stressed how tired he was. I talked to him the entire ride back to his house and he kept begging me to spend the night with him, but I still wasn't comfortable doing that yet and I didn't want to just jump back into that 'routine' with him. If I wanted things to change and be different for the better, I had to show him what I wanted. He said he just wanted to hold me, and that may have been true, and as much as I wanted to go over there to be held by him, I had to remain strong and make him earn my love instead of me just giving it to him so easily and so quickly. He was a little upset, but I believe he understood. It didn't stop him from making comments...*okay I see you don't love me anymore like you used to, but I still love you, but that's okay, you don't have to come over.* That was his way of making me feel guilty and before, it would work like a charm, but I was still remaining strong. We must have gone back and forth on the phone for about an hour until we finally hung up. It was close to midnight. I was so tired. I later texted Damon via the Internet and said, *'I love you! Now stop it!'* I waited for a response, but he was acting spoiled, so I shut down my computer and went to bed and I assumed he did too.

The next morning Damon called me from work, only he had mistakenly called Arielle.

"Thanks for doing what I asked you," he said.

"Huh? Okay," Arielle answered with confusion.

He thought he was talking to me and when I didn't call him back, he called again and this time I answered.

"Hey," I said with a smile.

"Why did you say that when I called you?" He questioned.

"Huh? Oh you were talking to Arielle, not me," I laughed.

"Oh, glad I didn't say anything nasty," he laughed.

For the next few months we got along great. So good I thought the roller coaster ride was over, but he sure fooled me. Carl called and told me that Damon and Mabel were still communicating. I was angry because that meant Damon didn't believe a word I said about her and he knew that I would never lie to him about something like that. What was really going on? I had Carl put me on three way with Mabel and I asked for her and she first said she wasn't there, then I stated that I wanted to discuss Damon and she then said in an almost knowing voice that it was something she didn't want to hear and asked what was it about and I told her to stop calling and texting him because he and I were still together and she stated that she was just friends, but I quickly brought to her attention that friends don't sleep with each other and she got as quiet as a mouse. Then I tried the reverse psychology bullshit saying that women always get it wrong whereas they confront the other woman instead of the man, but Carl told me it was her that was doing the initiating. I asked her to respect what I was saying and that I didn't know what she thought she was going to get from Damon or what she thought Damon had, but no, it was not gonna happen. She then strangely asked me if I was the one that had everything in my name pertaining to Damon's possessions and if I was the one in the pictures underneath his dresser and the one who wrote him the letters he had in his drawers.

I thought to myself, *'damn this bitch went all through his shit'*. Carl told me she was a snoop. Were there pictures underneath his dresser of his ex-wife and letters in his drawers from her? I pushed that to the side and told her that I heard all about how she operates and commenced to letting her know that I was not going to allow her to try to use my kids' father. I told her that he worked too damn hard for all that he has and I wasn't gonna let some hood rat take advantage of him. She spoke with a deep, raspy voice like she was drunk or just woke up and spoke with such ghetto talk that she didn't finish some of her word endings and she got offended quickly because I called her a hood rat and began shouting at me and telling me that she had the same thing he had if not more. *(I knew that was a damn lie per Carl.)* I called her out once again on her ways that I knew of, then she really got pissed and said that she can do what she wanted and for me not to tell her what to do then, just before she hung up, she yelled out *"you can have em!" That muthafucka gay anyway with that tramp stamp tat and big black dicks porno he got!"* and BAM! went the phone. Carl and I both was dead ass silent for a moment. He said, *"I'm not gonna touch that ma, just know that your better than all of that. She has no respect and that I was a poster child, she was nothing and so was Damon and to shut the door on both of them."* Carl said if Damon couldn't see by now how much I loved him, that he never would and to let him go. I asked Carl what he thought this whole thing was about because she just was not Damon's type comparing her to his ex-wife and myself. He said that *"he's using her for something."* It was beyond me as to why Damon would stoop so low. I caught myself protecting him yet again and he was still communicating with her.

Later that night, Damon called and the feeling in my stomach was that he talked to Mabel and sure enough he had *(but not for long, she would text him and he would not respond and eventually she stopped communication with him altogether and he never contacted her again).* He and I had some words back and forth. He was furious with me and we ended up speaking out of turn to each other in an awful exchange of words. Needless to say, it was completely and finally over between us once and for all, but after he got off work, he called again and was talking nice to me; as if our horrible mouth to mouth display never took place and he told me about him getting ready to cut his grass and other chores he planned on doing. I wasn't interested in even hearing his voice, let alone cared what he was doing.

We then hung up and he called back twenty minutes later and asked what I was doing because he wanted to have dinner. I declined stating I was getting ready to take a shower and that I was not hungry. He said okay, that was all he wanted to know and we hung up. My thoughts took me back to our shouting match and words that were spoken. The words from both sides were awful enough, but his words stayed with me and hurt me to the bone. They were so harsh and I said some terrible, awful things to him too and for him to bypass them made me think of the roller coaster ride and our conversation at our last dinner together. *'I'm just playing with you when we argue and you let me push your buttons,'* but the words he spoke said I was overweight, to fuck off, said I thought I was his girlfriend for two years, that nobody wanted me ever, that he doesn't want it anymore, he never wanted a relationship with me, I was a bitch that got her feelings hurt again...just way too harsh to be playing and that triggered my anger and my hurt feelings called him a drunk, an asshole, bipolar bastard, and immature hanging out with kids. I meant those words at that time because he cut me down so badly. He would act like it was a simple argument and think we should go back to us or his definition of not being in a relationship, whatever, only when it was convenient for him, but as soon as he would go back to thinking with the wrong head, he would start an argument to push me away and tell me I can't get mad because we are not together. I couldn't take it anymore. Enough was finally enough and I had to walk away for good.

When my heart finally lined up with my mind, I cried like a baby because I knew it was over for me with him. I loved him so much that I was actually trying to protect him from a woman he was trying to start a relationship with when still carrying on with me, gassing me up to believe we were going to take our relationship a step further like with the ring and the twins and we moving into his house like we discussed.

It was a terrible situation to be subjected to. I knew that I had to allow myself to go through this process full blown and let it burn so deep that I never go back to him again. I knew it was going to be hard and I knew I was going to miss him dearly, but I had to accept that what was being given to me wasn't love...it was ignorance, it was disrespect, it was abuse. He didn't love me and at times, I felt like he hated me. He didn't hesitate to let me know that he would never love me as much as he loves his ex-wife. *I was so tired of living in her shadow with him. She didn't even think twice about him because she made a new life for herself for the past 2.5 years with another man, which was the duration that she was out of Damon's life.* Damon even went as far as to tell Arielle that if he and I were to argue again, that she could always call on him for anything. Now from the past, whenever he would say something like that usually meant he was about to do something that would hurt me and it always had something to do with him being with another woman. He was so predictable now.

Being on that rollercoaster ride with Damon for so long made me dismiss everything and I learned to love this man unconditionally, putting myself through emotional abuse. I was feeling that emotional abuse too as my system was wearing me down inside and even though I took up a personal trainer with kickboxing three days a week, my mind was beginning to ooze stress and made me feel fatigued to the point that I didn't want to do anything, not even work or go to meetings. I was falling into a depression where my comfort zone was lying in my bed and crying, not eating, and just remained silent with my thoughts and nodded my head or spoke quietly in a sad voice to respond to my babies. I was going backwards and ceased going forward.

The situation was killing me softly and slowly and, although I had a good support system, depression was taking over and I felt every bit of it inch by inch, second by second. He was breaking me down in all aspects and he had no remorse because he continued to drain me for as long as I allowed him to. I would go through spurts of crying spells out of the blue. It was already hurting that I couldn't eat or sleep. I wanted to be with him so badly, but I didn't want what came with him. I wanted him to be right and do right that I would pray to God to make him right because I knew God could do anything so I would write down my prayers in regard to Damon of what I wanted him to be to me and how I wanted him to treat me. I had it bad and I would, without hesitation, bend over backwards for him and overlooked too much just to be with a man that never had any intentions on ever making a life with me in a committed relationship. I lost myself in him. I loved his heart beat. That's how much I loved him and I waited for him to love me. It was time for me to put an end to the cycle and get my strength back from an emotional, mental, physical and spiritual aspect. It was time to get back to me.

Once I truly got myself together and removed myself from the 'dreamy la-la land' over 'King', I built my mental and emotional strength of dealing with him on another level. Yes, we were still together as if we were a couple, but this time it was completely different for me because I severed my emotions from him. I could be around him and we do our same routine of staying nights at each others houses, cooking for one another and going out to dinner, doing activities with the children. All in all, we would still do for one another and take care of each other, but I was much stronger as strange as it may sound. The only reason for that was because I was not in love with him anymore. That was the difference. I loved him and still cared for him, but I was no longer 'in love' with him, but we went back to calling each other by our nicknames of "King and L."

I no longer had confidence in King's existence in my life anymore because of the many games he played, so I began to keep my options open and started communicating with other men via cell phone that lived in other states that I knew from my hometown, different states I used to live, and from my past. I would never consider anyone from my community because I knew everyone knew King and King knew everybody. Now I do have a few male friends locally that we may do lunch from time to time, but nothing beyond our friendship. My reasons for not dating anyone were because of the way I was still dealing with King. I didn't want to bring someone else into my mess and he still had my heart. I only utilized my options whenever King would disappear. I didn't do it too often even when he did act like an ass and disappear because my options always wanted to fly me and the twins to them or fly down to me, or just have us relocate to live with them, but I couldn't have that. They were no slouches either, they had credentials of Mayor, police officers, accounting executives, CEO/business owners, athletic club owners, etc., they were all single, some with kids and some without, and to top it off, they had their shit together. I was going to continue my connection with them all. At least I wasn't sleeping with any of them, which was the least I could say for King. He would beg to differ of course, but trusting him was nonexistent in my place with him. He had to earn it if he felt I was worth it.

As time passed on, living and accepting our routine, somewhere down the line, things had changed...for the better. Now I know I said that before, but this time it was something that wouldn't go away. Either God answered my written prayers about King or me and Arielle's prayers in regards to King, but his behavior began to alter. I would hear him randomly say, "thank you God!" I had no idea what he was thanking God for and I didn't want to ask, I was just happy that he was thanking Him and acknowledging Him. I would notice King staring at me oftentimes as if his mind went elsewhere with me in his deep thought process along with an endearing smile on his face. I would catch his eye and smile back and that's when I would receive a hug from him and not just an ordinary hug, a deep squeezing, affectionate embrace with kisses all over my face. He was displaying his love for me without words and I didn't mind, instead, I welcomed and treasured it.

For three years, I went through hell with this man. Now I don't recommend this type of relationship to anyone, not for one second. I allowed myself to get sucked back in regardless of what my foundation stood for. Although he didn't abuse me the way my ex-husband had as much physically, King still abused me emotionally and that was worse than a fist in my face. I got emotionally attached and it was my emotions that allowed me to continue to be abused by someone that didn't care for me and to be honest, I'm not so sure if he really cared for my kids because he didn't contact any of them whenever we were on the outs, except when it would be convenient for him after he had been drinking and asking my older girls to please have me call him and talk to him. I should have closed this door a long time ago. I should have put an end to it when I saw the first red flag. As much as I didn't want to be in a relationship from the beginning, I was fighting so hard to stay in this one. I didn't walk away. I was a hypocrite in a sense. I gave advice to domestic abuse survivors that came to my foundation, but I was living a lie.

18

Judgement Day

For he will command his angels concerning you to guard you in all your ways.

Psalm 91:11

The clock was winding down for the court appearance for Jason. Seems that "B's" mother wanted him to face at least 7 years of prison time, dropped from 10 to 15 years, and she also wanted to sue Damon in the process. Her reasoning for that was because Damon allowed them to drink before they all left his home and headed out to a club and, afterwards, on the way back to Damon's house, they were racing, which caused the accident along with being intoxicated. The case was getting ugly and it didn't look good for Jason, Damon or Aaron. The prosecutor received statements against Damon written by Myrtle stating that when she arrived at his house that night, everyone was already taking shots of vodka and they were racing on the way back. She stated that Damon was an alcoholic and allowed underage drinking at his house on a daily basis, as she witnessed it on several occasions. Myrtle also informed the prosecutor that Aaron was the one driving but Damon and Aaron wrote statements that night of the accident that Myrtle was driving, however, Damon and Aaron forgot that they had a recorded call the night of the accident that clearly indicated intoxication from the slurring of their voices, stating that Aaron was the driver. That wouldn't look good for Aaron, as his driver's license had been suspended since 2007/2008, of which he presently had an open case in court for. With Jason's life on the line, he had to tell the truth about what happened that night and the truth included Damon with the drinks already being at his house and the racing.

Damon didn't seem to care at all about the case because he continued to allow underage drinking in his house. Life was like a big party to him. I didn't understand his thought process at all. Maybe he felt like he was untouchable or he just didn't take it seriously. Not sure what was going through his mind, but it showed that he didn't care and that didn't sit too well with those that missed "B", especially her mother. Before our breakup, Damon told me that he and Aaron weren't the ones on trial, Jason was and, therefore, he had no concerns. Wrong attitude to have when you're supposed to be a friend. Jason had gone to school with Damon's sons, so they had known each other for a very long time. I think the question that was going to come up once the case was actually heard in court is "What was Damon doing with these 20 something year olds?" It was a question that people were beginning to already ask.

It didn't take long for friendships to sever. Damon's side of the story was that Jason stopped speaking to him and Jason's side of the story was that Damon stopped calling him once court proceedings began. Later on, Damon kicked Aaron out of the house for reasons, per Damon, "Aaron was telling Damon's business about what goes on in Damon's household," and it wasn't the first time according to Damon.

Another court date was set for October 31, 2012. There was exactly a week left until court and they have already had two continuances. Arielle and I made sure to attend for continued support and we didn't have anything to do with it but Damon or Aaron never showed up for any court dates. In fact, communications between Damon and Jason had ceased altogether shortly after the case went to court.

The day for court came and Arielle and I sat in a row next to Jason and his mother, all of us unsure if the lawyer was going to carry it out or ask for another continuance. We sat listening to other cases before Jason's was called. He walked up to the front to face the judge alongside his lawyer and that's when his lawyer requested one last continuance of the case. The judge granted his request and set the new date for December 5, 2012 at 9:00 AM. My thoughts were that if Jason's lawyer asked for 'one last' continuance, then on December 5th, maybe the judge was going to actually listen to the case and make a sentencing date another time or on that day. Shortly after, subpoenas were issued out and paperwork was drawn up on "B's" mother's behalf against Damon to sue him. I was definitely going to be there to show my support for everyone just like the last court date and from the sounds of it, Damon was going to be there too for this one. I believe that court date given was the sentencing for Jason. I wasn't sure what the outcome was going to be for Damon and Aaron, but I was soon to find out.

Thus far, it didn't look very good for either one of them, especially Damon because all the statements submitted to "B's" mother's attorney made him the center of the alcohol intake and it was done in his house along with a picture of Aaron and Jason holding liquor bottles by Damon's pool on his back patio. Her attorney received written statements from several of "B's" friends against Damon that he always allowed underage drinking in his home because they were underage at the time they visited him with "B" and he even drank with them. The attorney also retrieved a text message from "B's" cell phone that she texted a friend of hers that night stating that she was at Damon's house making a taco dinner for all of them and they were drinking shots about to go out to a club. "B's" mother was after whatever she could get from Damon. She was angry and was going for blood. She had plans of taking Damon for everything he had, but was starting with suing his house insurance first. It was all about to get ugly real fast in a matter of seconds from the judge's gavel hitting with permanent decision sentences.

December 5, 2012, court day, a new judge and another continuance, but just before that was granted, it was learned that Myrtle backed out and decided she was not going to testify, therefore, she was never subpoenaed. She just wanted to be left alone and "B's" mother had a change of heart and decided to let Damon off the hook in regards to suing him, but she went back to wanting Jason to do at least 7 years prison time.

January 9, 2013, court was early morning of 9:00 AM. The only people in the courtroom to the left were "B's" side of the family that consisted of her mother, brother and a handful of friends, and on the right side were Jason's mother, father, brother, friend, girlfriend, her aunt and myself. By the time I walked in, the judge was already talking to Jason who was standing next to his lawyer at the podium. Just before the judge read his charges off to him, "B's" mother and friend spoke about how good of a person "B" was and her mother, full of despair and tears, stated that she never thought she would have to have bury her only daughter. It was a sad moment indeed. Her friend then shared that she never would have imagined that she would be wearing "B's" ashes around her neck. Her ashes were inside of a trinket on the necklace. After the judge took their words into consideration, he then read Jason's charges off to him as to careless driving, not wearing a seatbelt, DUI manslaughter, DUI alcohol, DUI with property damage, and unlawful speeding of which he pled guilty to all charges. The judge then asked Jason if he wished to say anything and Jason stated that he was sorry about everything and then apologized to both his family, as well as "B's". Shortly after, the judge gave Jason a sentence of 5 years of imprisonment, 10 years probation and a suspension of his driver's license indefinitely. As soon as the judge hit his gavel, the sheriff asked for Jason's neck tie and belt, handcuffed him and then took him to the back where he was no longer visible.

19

❧

IT'S FINALLY OVER

Iron sharpens iron, and one man sharpens another.

PROVERBS 27:17

After three years of courtship, I thought King was finally settled. Our relationship had blossomed into something special. We had no more arguments or fights. We were a family. On occasions, we would drive to Orange County to visit my three oldest daughters, as they had all relocated for career choice purposes to another city. When we got together, it was wonderful. King would cook for them and then he would spend most of his visit playing with my grandson. He was known as "Grand PaPa" and my grandson adored him. When back at home, Damon would stay at my house for weeks at a time and the twins and I would stay at his house for weeks at a time. We were practically living together with our belongings stored at each others homes. We were a family. It was so nice to be in this place with him. We got along so beautifully on a daily basis and I'm not talking for just two or three months either. I felt like I was never going to go through all the nonsense again like in the past. He was settling and comfortable and I was enjoying it. No more 20 something kids hanging around being disrespectful.

At times, we would have friends over that were in our age range to play spades. *(Sometimes I didn't like to be his partner because he would always get pissed, embarrass, and yell at me and belittle me over the game if I didn't throw out a card he expected, but if I didn't have the card, I couldn't give him what he wanted.)* Besides that, a year went by of living in peace with one another. All was going so well until that one day. That one day when I called one of our friends and asked her if she could put braids in my baby girl's hair. She told me that she had carpal tunnel and couldn't but recommended Levi. I knew of Levi's work of doing hair and he was really good and, besides, he told me we were okay a few years ago, so I gave her permission to give him my number.

A day later, Levi called me.

"You still want me to do the baby's hair?" he inquired.

"Yes, please. How much do you charge?" I asked.

"About $25 to $30," he said.

"Okay, not bad. I will pick you up when they get out of school," I said.

"Okay then, just give me a call when you're ready," he said. Knowing the history between King and Levi, I didn't tell him right away who was doing baby girl's hair.

The next day I decided to give King a call just because. I waited until I knew he was off around 5 o'clock pm. When his cell rang, it had that little boop at the end, meaning he was on the phone, but he was not clicking over for me. So I thought to myself, I'm gonna play with him and when he clicks over I'm gonna tell him, "boy you know it was me" so I kept calling him back to back, but my joke didn't work out as planned. He was already pulling up to my house and when he came inside, he said to me in a firm voice, "What is wrong with you? Why do you have to call me over and over again just because I don't answer? I was on the phone with my mother!"

I apologized and told him I was just playing, but he was still angry. A bit much I thought. He always took his anger to another level for attention. I didn't want to give it to him, so I ignored his pouty mouth attitude and watched television with him and talked to him regarding the program we were watching just as normal routine and for his responses to me, he was head shaking or shoulder shrugging, not wanting to open his mouth to talk to me or look at me.

He carried this into bed, as he slept way over on the other side of my king sized bed. If I tried to touch him with just a foot, he would move over so I knew not to touch him anywhere else. The next morning, he still had the attitude, but I ignored it and began to make his breakfast as usual and lunch before his leaving for work. He was taking a little longer than normal before leaving out of my bedroom and when he did come out he had his laundry basket along with his other work clothes I ironed for the week that were in my closet and all his toiletries from my bathroom. He headed for the front door and said that he would talk to me later. I did not hear from him all that day. Normally, he would call me during work if he was free and chat and joke with me. It was silence all day and night.

The next day I still hadn't heard anything from King. I went about my work business as normal as time passed away. It was close for the twins to get off the bus. I called Levi to let him I was on my way to the bus stop to pick up the kids and from there, I was going to come around the corner to get him. He asked if it was okay if his friend could come along. I let him know it was okay with me. He then asked if I could drop his brother, Adam, off at work. While en route to dropping Adam off, Levi asked me about King and myself.

"So how you and Damon doing?" he inquired

"Better actually. He's been treating me much better, but you know how he gets every now and then when...." I tried to finish, but Levi finished my words for me and for a moment we were in unison. "When he gets drunk and gets an attitude, oh girl don't I know. I remem...." he caught himself and paused and jumped to..."Tell him that I want him to fry me some of that fish and make me some turkey spaghetti," he requested

"Yeah, I will," I answered.

'*Whoa!*' I thought to myself. He just took me back to the first year of when King and I were courting. His aura reeked of the past and I felt like I was living in it and the feeling was not good at all. When we got to my house, I began frying Tilapia for everyone. While Levi was good into braiding my baby's hair, I dispersed into my bedroom with King on my mind, so I called him just to start a conversation and told him that I saw Aaron on a moped the other day. King's response was nonchalant of '*yeah, so, I'm doing my floors, gotta go.*' It was obvious and clear that he didn't want to talk to me. I tried to hide in my voice the hurt and told him okay and we hung up. It appeared that he was still mad about the stupid phone call incident. I knew he carried grudges, but this was ridiculous and childish. I decided to call him again and this time, I told him that Levi was at my house putting braids in baby girl's hair. He had a little conversation then and his tone of voice changed from dead to alive.

"Yeah?...okay." he said.

"Okay, I was just telling you. So far it looks good," I said.

"How long was he over there?" he inquired.

"Since 4:30ish. Hey your dad is here. I saw him. You still doing your floors?" I asked.

"Oh, I didn't know he was in town. Yeah, I'm still doing my floors. Okay, talk to you later." He hung up.

I remember thinking as I sat at the end of my bed, '*now if he was on the phone with his mother that day when I was calling his phone, then how did he not know his dad was in town? His mother always calls him and tells*

him when his dad is in town...such a liar! He wasn't talking to his mother'.
Twenty minutes later, he was walking through my door. I heard the kids
saying *'hey Daddy'*. I thought to myself, I know I didn't just hear them say
Daddy. Yes I did. I heard King talking to Levi, asking him questions of
how is he doing and where has he been and where is he living now and
with his soft voice, Levi was answering his questions. Then Levi told him
that I fried some fish, and then added that it didn't taste like King's fish.

"I know. She knows she can't cook like me," King boldly and loudly
replied.

At this point, King came back to my bedroom where I was sitting at
the end of my bed watching the news. He sat in the chair next to my bedroom door where you could see out into the family room in view of Levi
doing baby girl's hair. King kept looking out there, but talking to me, asking how long was Levi doing her hair and I reminded him that I told him
earlier. His whole demeanor was different and not of the person I knew of
as recent. I couldn't connect with his spirit any longer. It was shaded and
strange. He acted as if he didn't know how to act around me. Like he was
nervous and was a bit rude to me in speaking in normal conversation. It
was in his tone, like his questions were being asked with an attitude. He
seemed to not know what to say to me. My spirit didn't set right with him.
His behavior took me back to the first year of our courtship too when all
the bullshit with him and Levi took place. I began to pay close attention,
as I was not going to dismiss the nonsense anymore, especially since my
feelings for King had changed tremendously. *I loved him unconditionally
back then and dismissed the signs and text messages I saw and heard about
between him and Levi.* I walked out of my room with him following behind me and I sat on the couch making small talk with Levi's guy friend.

At that moment, King lit incense, something he would do just before he
would smoke a cigarette in the house to take away the cigarette smell. Levi's
friend asked what was the name of the incent and I loudly answered 'frank-
incense & myrrh' but King felt compelled to take the packet over to Levi, who
did not ask and was still doing baby girl's hair and showed him the package.
Levi then read the name out loud and his friend replied with how good it
smelled. I was a fucking ghost in the room. At this point, I went to look for
my son, whom seemed to disappear. I went into his room and there he was
lying across his bed watching his TV with a look of disgust on his face.

"What's wrong Baby?" I asked.

"Is he still out there?" he asked.

"Who?" I inquired.

"That guy who sounds like a girl," he replied

"Yes Baby, he's still doing your sister's hair. Why? You want him to
leave?" I asked.

"I'm going to Jerry's?" he informed me with a question mark.

"Go ahead," I permitted, as I watched him skateboard out through the garage, down the street with a fish sandwich in his hand.

"Be back before dark," I yelled

"Yeeeessss maaa'aaam!"

I sat back on the couch with King's stank aura. I was beginning to feel disgusted because I was thinking back that he made it clear by the tone of his voice that he did not want to see me at all tonight and he still had an attitude with me about the stupid ass phone call. So why was he at my house? Then I started getting mad at the same time as I was going through my thought process and this bastard was not talking to his mom on the phone that day, then hanging up just before he hit my front door. If that was his mother on the phone, he would have stayed on the phone and told her hello for me or let me talk to her so I can say it to her myself and if he was talking to his mother, he would have known that his dad was in town and now, he was sitting on my couch acting like he had a damn crush and it wasn't on me. He was acting nervous and his conversation with me was off like he didn't know what to talk about while we were watching one of our usual detective documentaries. Then he could barely look me in the face because he knew he was just being an ass to me an hour beforehand.

Time was getting past us and my lil' man just popped back home. Levi had just finished my baby's hair and she looked so beautiful. He did a really good job. I told him that I would like for him to keep it up on an every two week basis and he agreed that it would be fine with him. I paid him and he gave me a hug and stated that he was going to walk home back to his mother's house, as they only lived less than five minutes away driving and about 15 minutes walking. I informed him that I would take him home and before I could finish the 'me' on 'home', King interrupted me and jumped up, grabbed his cigarettes, and said, "Oh I'm leaving, I'll take you home." And then he quickly walked out through the garage door with Levi and his friend following closely behind. He then asked me while hauling ass pass me, "What you gonna do?"

"Huh?" I asked.

"What you gonna do? You coming or what?" he inquired.

"I'll call you," I said as I was closed my garage door.

What in the hell was that about? I did exactly what I said I was going to do. I paid attention to my surroundings and I didn't dismiss anything and I saw what I needed to see. While everyone was here, I had already said a silent prayer asking God to give me discernment in their presence and He did just that. I was not seeing things and my imagination was not running wild and I was not looking too deep or looking for anything. My mind was clear with understanding of everything I had witnessed. Twenty minutes later, King texts me.

"I asked you what you gonna do?"

"It was nice seeing Levi again huh?" I texted.

Instead of receiving a text back, he called. "Hey, I asked you what you gonna do?" he again repeated, yelling in a happy voice, as there was loudness in the background.

"What is that noise?" I asked.

"I don't know, I'm standing under my TV I guess," he said.

"Naw, I'm good," I replied.

"You're not coming?" he said sadly.

"No. The twins are in bed," I said.

"Okay. Alright then, bye." He hung up sadly.

A few minutes later, I texted him my feelings.

ME: "You just took me by surprise when you didn't want me to come over to your house earlier. You had no plans on coming over to mine until I told you that Levi was at my house. You stopped doing your floors and you pop up and all of a sudden you want me and the twins to stay the night. Then to top it off, you jumped up to take him home as if he was the only reason why you came over," I texted

HIM: "That's not true," he texted back with not much else to say.

ME: "Can you put yourself in my shoes please. Imagine how that looked to me, especially knowing ya'll's history," I countered

HIM: "You're so stupid you know that," he argued

ME: "I'm not stupid anymore. I got my eyes wide open."

HIM: "Good! Then you saw everything. BYE!" he replied.

ME: "What?!" I texted with no reply from him.

The next day after I knew he was off of work, I texted him and said dinner was ready and that I bought him a small bottle of vodka and beer and wine for myself so we could watch a movie tonight. He didn't respond. I waited for at least 30 minutes and I called him this time.

"Hey, you get my text message?" I asked.

"Yeah I got it," he replied back in the same tone of voice as he had used the day before when he told me he was doing his floors.

"Well why didn't you respond?" I inquired.

"I didn't want to," he said.

"What's the problem? I know you're not still mad about yesterday? Come on. We should be able to talk about anything and everything and we should be able to relay to each other how we feel about things without holding grudges or getting mad. So stop being mad. Are you going to come over?" I asked.

"No! I don't want to. I'm doing my hardwood floors," he said.

"Well I will bring everything over there then," I insisted.

"No! Don't come over here. I can't do my floors with you here," he added.

"What are you talking about? You did the floor plenty of times with me and the kids there and I helped you," I reminded him.

"Well I don't want you here now. I gotta go," he replied and hung up.

I texted him and said, 'I'm coming anyway'. My kids went to our neighbors' house to play while I went to King's house to see what the real problem was. When I got to the door, I rang the doorbell several times before he answered.

"What the hell are you doing here? Didn't I say I don't want to see you?" he said angrily.

"Well I don't listen very well and I want to see you," I replied while still standing at his front door.

"Well I don't want to see you do you understand that? I don't want to see you or talk to you so leave!" he commanded, trying to close the door on me.

"No! Not until you tell me what the problem is," I demanded.

"It's over! I'm done with you! I'm finished! No more back and forth!" he said while not even looking in my direction.

"What?! Why?!" I cried.

"You and Levi's history, what the hell is that?" he asked.

"You know what I'm talking about from the past. The text messages and you told me so yourself and I heard it from Levi's mouth," I added.

"You're so stupid! You're so fuckin dumb! You believe everything that is told to you. Just get out!" he shouted.

"I'm not leaving until you tell me the real reason why you're breaking up with me because just last night, you wanted me and the twins to stay the night," I reminded him. "When did you decide this?" I asked.

"Just now!" he paused.

"That makes no sense. What changed in 24 hours King?"

"I changed. People change. I can change my fucking mind, now get out of my house or I'm calling the police!" he said reaching for his cell phone.

"I'm not leaving until you talk to me like a fucking man!" I demanded.

"I'm done talking! Give me back my garage door opener and here is the key to your house!" he said.

"I knew it. I knew this was going to happen. For almost our entire third year together, we had been getting along beautifully and lately, you have been having these sneaky phone calls and text messages from a woman in your past and now Levi pops back up, you switch up. I knew this was gonna happen. I was waiting for this," I said.

He remained quiet and turned away from me and looked down at his phone as if to call 911. Then he comes out of no where, "Well go ahead and tell everybody everything like you always do!" he said.

"What are you talking about? I did that three years ago and have not done it since and why would you say that?" I asked confused.

"You're just fucking crazy and twisted. You write your fucking books and tell lies and live in this made up world! You're delusional!" he said.

"What the hell are you talking about King? What is wrong with you?" I screamed with tears in my eyes.

"Just what the hell are you talking about anyway saying that I told you something? What did I tell you?" he demanded.

"You told me that the real reason why your ex-wife left you was because she found out you were with another man and then another time you told me that when Levi 'put it in' you made a wwwoooo sound. You say a lot of things when you've been drinking King," I explained. "Drunk man tell no tales right. Ain't that what you always told me?" I asked.

"Well if you believe that then you're fucking stupid! Get out!" He said.

"You know it's true. I can't make up shit like that. Where would I begin and where could I get it from? And I already told you about the time that Levi told me that he came to you letting you know that he had a crush on you. I asked you to see if it was true and you told me that it was with a stupid ass side smile on your face. I'm sorry, but I can't make up shit like that," I said.

"Are you ashamed? If so, I understand." I said.

"I'm not ashamed of anything I do! And if you thought I was with Levi then why did you stay?!" he yelled.

"Because I loved you unconditionally!" I said.

It was complete silence. He stopped and looked at me with a surprised look on his face.

"Just leave!" he demanded as he began dialing 911, telling the police my name, my license plate information, and telling them that I was his ex-girlfriend and I refused to leave his house.

I gave up and he watched me storm out to my car, listening to every word I yelled and screamed of how he was gonna get it all back and that karma was real. When I got into my car, started it, and proceeded to back out, I looked at him one last time and then he taunted me with smirks on his face and half smiles. I abruptly put my car in park, got out to yell at him and he started running back toward his front door telling the operator that I was trying to attack him. I called my eldest daughter Lisa and told what was going on and she begged me to just leave, that he was trying to keep me there for when the cops came to have me arrested. She screamed for me to go home and be with the twins. She reminded me that he was who he was and to let him go. I drove off the opposite way from leaving his house with the thought that I would pass the police had I went my normal way. When I passed by the opposite of his street, I saw the police zoom by. Lisa stayed on the phone with me until I assured her that I was home safe and that the twins were with me. I told her that we were all just fine and she began to tell me that he was not worth all that I have worked for. She was absolutely right. We hung up after saying our *'love you's'* and I put the twins to bed and I stayed up to the break of dawn. Hurt and anger would not allow me to sleep a wink...I needed closure.

20

❧

NEW BEGINNINGS

Be ye not unequally yoked together with unbelievers: for what fellowship hath righteousness with unrighteousness? And what communion hath light with darkness?

2 CORINTHIANS 6:14

As bad as I wanted to call him, I didn't, although he was heavy on my mind. The, just as I was thinking about him, he texted me, asking if I was home. I didn't respond because it was too soon. Less than 24 hours ago, he had just told me we were over and there was no back and forth and then he called the cops on me to have me arrested per his words. I was confused. One side of me wanted to respond because I wanted to be with him again. The other side of me wanted it to be over to so I refused to respond because I believed he just wanted to get rid of me for that night. We had plans to watch the UFC girl fight at his house. I even had it marked down on his calendar. This was something that we had planned together a few weeks back. I still wanted to see the fight, so I called a few friends to come over to my house to watch it on pay per view. Just as I was figuring out what I was going to serve my friends, Levi called. Why would he be calling me now? I told him that I was going to call him in two weeks when it was time to redo baby girl's hair. I didn't trust myself so I didn't answer and he didn't leave any messages. If he and King were playing the same games as in the past, I was not going to be apart of it anymore. I started looking at my social media page and I began to post about the fight, then I updated my foundation page with the events we had coming up and the guest appearances I was going to be doing on news stations and radio shows. Right after I posted, King right away put a thumbs up. He had it fixed where whenever I posted or commented or did anything either to my page or someone else's, it would give him a buzz on his cell phone. I didn't acknowledge his thumbs up. I signed off and moved on with my plans with my friends for the evening.

The next morning, it was still bugging me as to why King broke up with me so I made a fake social media page and friend requested him. I figured that since he couldn't be honest with me about us; he would be honest with another woman. I made the page and found pictures of a white girl *(his preference per him, as he would say, 'black women were bitches – accept for me per him, as he felt that my skin complexion was so light that I had white in me')* so I found the dirtiest in appearance, less fortunate white woman pictures I could find on the internet and made a social media page out of it. I went to his page and friend requested him and quickly, he accepted. I made conversation with speaking illiterate and misspelling words on purpose:

Fake Page / Kathy 11:05am: Thanks for the add. Looking at your page you ride horses how nice. i rode years ago at my uncles farm.
Him 11:06am: Might go again next week
Fake Page / Kathy 11:07am: how cool. that yur girlfriend you were riding with? sorry if being nosy lol
Him 11:08am: No . I work with her .
Fake Page / Kathy 11:08am: oh ok where yall work at?
Him 11:10am: Rock Advantage
Fake Page / Kathy 11:11am: heard of that. like stuff you can buy for your yard
Him 11:11am: Yes
Fake Page / Kathy 11:12am: nice. what you up to today? look like rain to me. might take my litle girl out to the park
Him 11:12am: What park
Fake Page / Kathy 11:14am: regents i think is close i was told by a school? why you coming lol
Him 11:16am: I might . Lol . What section you live in ?
Fake Page / Kathy 11:16am: w i dont do drama. you got a girlfriend? be truthful because most guys aint
Him 11:17am: Just broke up fri . Lmao
Fake Page / Kathy 11:18am: oh why is that ok to ask i saw a lady on your page said she was with you doing pedi's is that her

Him 11:19am: Yes
Fake Page / Kathy 11:18am: pretty. yall still friends you didnt delete her.
Him 11:21am: Not friends now but maybe later
Fake Page / Kathy 11:21am: how long were you together
Him 11:19am: 3 years
Fake Page / Kathy 11:22am: yall got kids twins good amount of time. still love her i know
Him 11:23am: They are hers but I call them mine .
Fake Page / Kathy 11:23am: oh thats nice. good guy lol still love her miss her. i miss my dautghrs dad
Him 11:24am: like her yes
Fake Page / Kathy 11:24am: 3 years an you like her lol. how does that work how can you be with sombody for 3 years and only like them lol
Him 11:26am: Lmao it work
Fake Page / Kathy 11:26am: then your heart must be elsewhere because thats a long time or your just cold hearted lol
Him 11:26am: What time you going to the park ?
Fake Page / Kathy 11:31am: dunno yet you like to ignore questions lol i will stop asking ok does she only like you and not love you
Him 11:32am: Let me know I might stop by . I don't know . Lmao
Fake Page / Kathy 11:32am: i aonly ask because my little girls dad acts like cold too sometimes
Him 11:32am: Where is he at
Fake Page / Kathy 11:34am: i just trying to figure out why men act like that. she must tell you she love you in 3 years. i told him all the time and he would say it back and i think he meant it most times lol hes around back and forth in enola and bestol and here do you love her kids
Him 11:36am: Yes
Fake Page / Kathy 11:36am: lol wait dumb ass question you cant if you dont love they mom no way lol i dont believe that one lol you dont love they momma but you love them. sorry but that dont work why was you with her then
Him 11:39am: You ask too many questions . Lol
Fake Page / Kathy 11:40am: lmao you must love her because you dont like to answer questions lol are you a guy that only love baby mommas kids but only like the moms? (*I said this because I remember him saying that he went with women who had children to make that woman and those children feel wanted...who was he to decide that they didn't feel wanted?!*) Lol where do you live because you asked me where i lived. is that an okay question lol
Him 11:43am: The d section .
Fake Page / Kathy 11:44am: oh you must like that question lol hey my lil

girls dad is texting me can we talk later. you have a number? i only have this and a text phone leave me your number and i will text you later if that is ok text you when i go to park ok
Him 11:46am: 8412159
Fake Page / Kathy 11:47am: k bye for now
Him 11:47am: K

I was blown away at his answers to this fake person. He actually told her that he *'liked'* me when she asked if he still loved me. In his reply, he thought it to be funny when she asked how did that work to be with someone for three years and only like them...'it works' he said. Wow! My anger wouldn't allow me to stop. Since the fake person told him that she would call him later, I got online and searched for fake numbers and found one that would allow you to text as well. I waited until later on in the evening before having this fake person contact him. In the meantime, he contacted me with a phone call, but I didn't answer. I was too upset and would have blown my cover, so I let it ring.

After I got the fake number situated, I texted him:

Fake # / Kathy 5:12pm: hey its Kathy from social media. hey didnt go to the park after all. my lilttle girls daddy came over.
Him 5:12pm: That's good . I was busy today . Help a friend in his yard got my taxes done and cleaned the house .
Fake # / Kathy 5:13pm: you was busy lol what you doing tonight
Him 5:14pm: Getting ready for work . Why what's up ?
Fake # / Kathy 5:15pm: just asking. you sound like you want company lol
Him 5:16pm: Lol ! Naw I got 2 meetings tomorrow . Gonna be a long day . In bed early tonight .
Fake # / Kathy 5:17pm: ok just checking lol. maybe another time about to get me and my baby something to eat
Him 5:18pm: Tomorrow ! Lmao
Fake # / Kathy 5:19pm: tomorrow ok i'm gonna hold you to it lol you said you live in the d area?
Him 5:19pm: I just came from mezzanine didn't feel like cooking.
Fake # / Kathy 5:19pm: where about
Him 5:20pm: Off Dyer
Fake # / Kathy 5:19pm: is that by regents whats your address
Him 5:21pm: Yes 354 devlin road . And yours ?
Fake # / Kathy 5:22pm: no ex girlfriend come around is she lol what time tomorrow i live with my aunt. she is not to fond of anyone who aint white know what i mean but i will come by when you give me a time
Him 5:23pm: I get off at 5:30 I understand .

Fake # / Kathy 5:25pm: come by then or 6 give you time to get in my baby dad is black and peurto rica. is anyone gone pop up ex girl

Him 5:27pm: About 6 . Will text tomorrow when I get home . Maybe a drive by . Lmao

Him 5:28pm: Are you still working at blue crabs ? How old are you?

Fake # / Kathy 5:28pm: yeah nights..old eanuff. you look older tho but thats okay. who drive by your ex girl? will she knock if she see extra cars

Him 5:30pm: My ex lol ! How old are you ? No she won't knock .

Fake # / Kathy 5:31pm: over 25 lol. you sure. yal just broke up she might get jealous i dont want no trouble had my ass kicked by black girl few times lol not fun

Him 5:33pm: I'm sure . What's over 25 ? 26 ?

Fake # / Kathy 5:34pm: somewhere around there. what you gone do to me when i come over

Him 5:34pm: I am a lot older ! Lol

Fake # / Kathy 5:34pm: is that a problem for you

Fake # / Kathy 5:34pm: can you answer my questions please lol

Him 5:35pm: I'm not going to do anything . Lol . No problem for me . Send me a pic

Fake # / Kathy 5:38pm: cant this cell so old lol. can only do texting. baby daddy gift asshole he is if i make a move on you your not gone do anything

Him 5:38pm: No I'm a real man ! Lol

Fake # / Kathy 5:38pm: ok then but if i start touching you just gone let me and not do nothing real men get aroused to lol

Him 5:41pm: How tall are you ? I'm short with a big attitude ! Lmao

Fake # / Kathy 5:41pm: bout 5 ft 4in. how short

Him 5:41pm: Doesn't mean I have to do anything . I'm 5'3"

Fake # / Kathy 5:43pm: 5 3 not bad. if i pull it out and suck your dick your not gone do anything lol

Him 5:44pm: Nope! Lmao

Fake # / Kathy 5:44pm: you lie lol im sucking your dick your girl drive by knocks or call what you gone do lol

Him 5:45pm: Sit there ! Lol

Fake # / Kathy 5:46pm: why men lie lol that scares me i dont want anothe ass whoopin black girls can fight and i cant lol sorry

Him 5:47pm: I got you .

Fake # / Kathy 5:47pm: any chance yal get back together

Fake # / Kathy 5:48pm: helo

Him 5:48pm: No not for me . It wasn't working out . I'm divorced been there before .

Fake # / Kathy 5:49pm: how you got me you gone beat her ass for me lol

Him 5:50pm: No wont answer door .
Fake # / Kathy 5:50pm: lol okay. she might want you back tho right. don't want to get inmiddle of nothing
Him 5:51pm: Gotta go my son is here . I'll text when he leaves .
Fake # / Kathy 5:51pm: you must been tellin the truth when you said you dont love her...ok

At this time, I wanted to see if the fake number worked so I called his cell phone and he answered sounding drunk, speech slurred. I was trying to listen to the background, but couldn't hear much.

Fake # / Kathy 8:19pm: Sorry about that
Fake # / Kathy 8:19pm: You sound likr you having fun
Fake # / Kathy 8:22pm: son still there. call me later and i wil come over
Him 8:23pm: Just chillin son and his daughter here . Will call when they leave .
Fake # / Kathy 8:25pm: Ok. Would like to be your next girlfriend
That is if your looking ...Are you?
Him 8:28pm: You don't even know me yet . I will call when they leave .
Fake # / Kathy 8:30pm: Ok. Text instead. My baby will be sleeping Ok. Text instead. My baby will be sleeping
Him 8:30pm: K . How u comin over if the baby sleep ?
Fake # / Kathy 8:33pm: My aunt will watch hwr
Fake # / Kathy 8:33pm: Her. Can I stay the night
Him 8:35pm: K . Wool text soon .
Fake # / Kathy 8:35pm: is that a yes i can or no
Him 8:36pm: Will text when they leave
Fake # / Kathy 8:39pm: you dont kno me yet but we gone fuck so whats the diff?
Him 8:39pm: K
Him 8:39pm: O . K . There gone . What you gonna do . Lol
Fake # / Kathy 8:41pm: what you mean. im stayn all night
Him 8:43pm: Hello
Fake # / Kathy 8:49pm: im stayin all night ? hello lol
Him 8:49pm: Well. Where you at
Fake # / Kathy 8:52pm: yes or no. i got a ride
Him 8:52pm: Yes
Fake # / Kathy 8:53pm: and if your ex bitch pop up then what?
i gotta daughter to go home to
Him 8:53pm: To late . Not !
Fake # / Kathy 8:54pm: dont want trouble from no bitches. what you mean to late?

Him 8:55pm: K .
Fake # / Kathy 8:55pm: what you mean to late. just dont want no bitches in my face i be there. bringing my razor
Him 8:55pm: To late for her to come by . What u gonna do
Fake # / Kathy 8:56pm: still gone bring my razor for her ass. she pretty bitch but i cut her face the fuck up. be there soon let me talk to my aunt
Him 8:56pm: K
Fake # / Kathy 8:59pm: dont get mad if shit go down because she done came by and i slice her ass lol you said you got me so
you should help me and not her
Him 8:59pm: Lol ! Not . I got you ! Come on !
Fake # / Kathy 8:59pm: okay so if you just gone let me beat her ass and cut her face the fuck up then you dont love that bitch no more lol
Him 9:00pm: Never did love . Just like . Where you at ?
Fake # / Kathy 9:00pm: hold on
Him 9:01pm: Yea O. K .

At this point, I was floored and my feelings were beyond hurt to see that he said that he didn't love me. This time, he elaborated and said he 'never did love' me, just 'liked' me. I had to take a moment to digest it all, not doing a very good job of holding back tears. My heart sank and I began to shake. I just sat there staring at his words of 'never did love, just like'...it hit me hard. I remembered the times that he had told me that he loved me and just recently when we went to hang out with his friend Grady, he told me he loved me. Now to know that he really didn't mean it at anytime that he has ever said it to me....I was crushed.

Fake # / Kathy 9:46pm: said i gone talk to my aunt now hold on. im gone suck that dick lol
Him 9:46pm: No your not .
Fake # / Kathy 9:47pm: she on the john hold on...and yes i am
we gone fuck
Him 9:48pm: Lol ! Your sick !
Fake # / Kathy 9:49pm: you gone fine out
Him 9:50pm: Do you drink ? Stop playin .
Fake # / Kathy 9:51pm: hell yea i drink anything. you drink
Him 9:51pm: Where you at ?
Fake # / Kathy 9:52pm: s section. i done told you already
Him 9:52pm: All day !!!!
Fake # / Kathy 9:49pm: huh
Him 9:52pm: I will come get you !
Fake # / Kathy 9:54pm: i done told you how my aunt is. she dont take kind

to who aint white my baby daddy is black he nigger all day to her lol she call me nigger lover

Fake # / Kathy 9:55pm: sorry i ofend you

Him 9:55pm: You can't offend me . Lol

Him 9:57pm: Going to wash these nuts and go to bed . Your playing !

Fake # / Kathy 10:03pm: wake up when i knock on your door

Him 10:03pm: K . Don't believe you .

The next day:

Him 5:19pm: What's up ?

Fake # / Kathy 5:22pm: Wassup wit u

Him 5:22pm: I'm home .

Fake # / Kathy 5:23pm: k

We did not contact each other anymore after that. Later on, I spent half the night figuring out how I was going to tell him. I definitely wanted to confront him, so I decided to send him an email copy of the entire transcript and wait for his response.

Email: The only reason why I did this was to get answers on why you threw me away. This is the only thing I ever did to you to find out the truth of why, and how I loved you and treated you good, you still threw me away and I got it...you just don't love me and I can't make you...(I then inserted the entire transcript.)

He sent me a text message instead of responding by email.

Him: Good job! Had good news in the AM. But you didn't answer. Love the insert from the book!

Me: Didn't do any new writing.

Me: Call Kathy Hamilton *(fake person)*.

Him: Just sign my book when it is finished. Got a big donation for it.

Me: Then the good job part must mean you got ur emails. Yeah okay bout the book.

Him: You are good! Lmao!

Him: Lmao!!!!

Him: When are we getting married? I can't run from you! Lmao! Lmao !

Me: Yeah laugh it up you say good jokes.

Him: What?!

Me: Your laughing and joking on me at my expense. You don't love me and never will. I know this now.

Him: No I'm not!

Me: You don't want to marry me. If you did, the twins and I would have been living in your house.

Him: I don't love anyone and I told you that along time ago! Can't live with anyone.

Me: Wish you could have told me you weren't serious all the times you did tell me you loved me.

Me: My strength has not overcome me as of yet. Hurting severely. I can't put into words.

Him: You went against me along time ago! When you did stuff behind my back! All the phone calls to every one else. And the texts! Your business is yours and mine is mine! Not for the streets!!!!

Me: What ur saying holds no weight. That was three years ago that whenever we broke up, I would call our friends. You harbor hate and hold grudges. Fact of the matter is, you were gonna allow someone to hurt me, slice my face up and then you told them you had their back against me. No matter what we went through, we always made up and I still protected you at the end of the day. And I tell you what, Damon, never would I ever have allowed anyone to harm u in such a way or slice ur face up and have their back against u. Especially not a stranger. Instead of denying that you would do that, you countered it with some nonsense. My ex-husband and twins' dad didn't hate me like that.

Him: You see things your way and your way only! Ask yourself why a strong black, intelligent woman like yourself is alone!

Me: I'm not alone. I was with you for 3 years. I put men off bcuz of u. Now that I'm single...when I'm ready, I will be with someone bcuz I am a beautiful, intelligent black woman.

Him: K

Me: I'm a black woman and bcuz a black woman damaged u...u made me pay for it that's why you go for low lifes. I'm sorry your ex-wife hurt you so bad that you lost yourself. I mean that with everything inside of me. I believe you to be a pretty good man that's why I stuck around in hopes that you would see me and not your past. I'm not Alice, I'm Quiet Storm and I loved you 110%.

Him: Think about how many people hurt you and why! Look in the mirror!

Me: Ur so hurt and full of pain and anger that you still choose to be nasty to me. Ur words aren't hurting me bcuz I know the pain it's coming from. You don't stop me from praying for you bcuz u need healing.

The next day, I decided to move to an undisclosed location unbeknownst to Damon for the safety of my children and myself due to a disturbing phone call I received out of my sleep around 10:30pm.

A loud uneducated in speaking female called my cellphone yelling and screaming, calling me a bitch multiple times and said that my daughters and I have been prank calling her phone per Damon. She said a few more choice words, as I was unable to get a word in edge wise then hung up. I called Damon and he would not respond to my calls or text. So I called the woman back and she would not answer as well, then I received a text message from her threatening to come to my house and beat my ass, then she texted me my address, stated what the names of both my companies were, then stated where and what city my three oldest daughters lived, and said she knew how old my twins were and that they lived with me, then she texted me my full name, and included my nickname. That was it for me with Damon. The next day, I spoke to a Realtor to relocate. For those that know me, know that I have no fear of man, woman or child, but with having my foundation, and being in the public eye like I was, the last thing I needed was to get into any type of altercation with anyone, especially over a man. I reported the text messages to our local police station and they gave Damon a call at his job the following morning and warned him that if anything happened to me or my children, that they were going to pay him a visit.

A few days later, I packed the rest of his belongings that I found in my house and put them in a box and set them in his driveway when I knew he would be at work to avoid any contact. He still had a ladder of mine that he boldly told me beforehand that he was not giving back (even though he had two) and for me to buy another one, so I wrote that off and decided to let it all go and move on.

We have not spoken since then, but have seen each other in passing without speaking. I then heard through the grapevine that Damon was pretty pissed that I had the police call his job and from that he stated, "fuck me and he never cared anything about my kids". What a blow that was for me and my children, as I let them know exactly what was said so if they ever saw him again, he could not be fake with them anymore.

It certainly has been a journey and hard lessons learned along the way. I never thought that in the three years of my life I spent with this man that it would end on such a horrible, scarred note. It was time to heal on both sides. Damon had issues way before he met me and he carried them into our relationship. I felt like he took the pain of his ex-wife leaving him out on me. I didn't want to be his enemy, but I didn't want to continue being his fool either. It was time for that horrible cycle to end. I wasn't strong enough to be his friend and actually hang out with him because we would have slipped back into our unhealthy routine. It was best at this time for me to keep my distance. After getting tested for STDs and HIV/AIDS (which came up negative for all) I began going to church like I know

I needed to even when I was with Damon, but I never did because that was something he just didn't do...church. Since our departure, business has progressed, the children are growing nicely, and I've come to know myself again.

Whether Damon knows it or not, I have learned a lot from him. He has taught me to not take any shit, so to speak, from anyone pertaining to business and my life in general. He has taught me to stay healthy in a sense of continuing to stay away from pork and indulge in chicken, fish and turkey, salads, etc. All of my children and I adopted this from him. He has taught me that if there is something that I absolutely want and need, and if I am able to financially, to not think about it, but to get it. He would always say, 'if you can get it, then get it, so you won't wish you had later." He has taught me to listen carefully to the choice of words people use and to not trust anyone, including him, because people are out to get something. I wish Damon well. I will always care for him and continue to pray for him. Lord willing, he would welcome healing to release the hurt from his past, not hold grudges, and leave that depressant of alcohol alone, and just began to live. With this book, I have closed a chapter in my life. I have taken the necessary steps to heal by forgiving and moving on...I look forward to new beginnings.

Bear with each other and forgive one another if any of you has a grievance against someone. Forgive as the Lord forgave you.

COLOSSIANS 3:13

This book should be used as a 'reflection'. A reflection not just to the man that I chose to call 'King' but to all men like him. When God blesses you with another chance at love, recognize it, embrace it, love on it, and respect it. Sometimes people do not comprehend words being released by mouth to ear, but when words are placed into action of being in black and white to read; they can finally see the hurt that was received from them to you and only then you can be heard. The chapters told in this book are unfortunately all true and I have no regrets of sharing my life with Damon.

After two decades of marriage, I was told I wasn't loved anymore, and now, I was told goodbye and I learned that I was never loved. I fell to my knees and cried out to God and He heard my cries and dried my tears. He said weeping may endure for a night, but joy comes in the morning. He said I'm Beautiful! I'm Smart! I'm Fabulous! I'm Fearless! I'm Focused! I'm Fearfully and Wonderfully Made! I'm Protected! I'm Successful! I'm Blessed!

Thank you Jesus for loving me unconditionally!

www.ingramcontent.com/pod-product-compliance
Lightning Source LLC
Chambersburg PA
CBHW052038270326
41931CB00012B/2538